A Practical ... for Divine Services

Compiled, translated and edited by
Father Gregory Woolfenden

from *Pravoslavnoe Bogosluzhenie* by I. V. Gaslov and
other Russian Orthodox liturgical sources

Holy Trinity Publications
The Printshop of St Job of Pochaev
Holy Trinity Monastery
Jordanville, New York

Printed with the blessing of His Eminence,
Metropolitan Hilarion, First Hierarch
of the Russian Orthodox Church Outside of Russia

A Practical Handbook for Divine Services
© 2011 Holy Trinity Monastery

Second Printing 2021

HOLY TRINITY PUBLICATIONS
The Printshop of St Job of Pochaev
Holy Trinity Monastery
Jordanville, New York 13361-0036
www.holytrinitypublications.com

ISBN: 978-0-88465-191-8 (Paperback)
ISBN: 978-0-88465-203-8 (Epub)

Library of Congress Control Number 2010940796

For Igumen Gregory – Memory Eternal!

IGUMEN GREGORY (Woolfenden) was born in 1946 in Liverpool, United Kingdom. His given name was Graham. Brought up in the Roman Catholic Church, he obtained degrees in philosophy and theology at the Pontifical Gregorian University in Rome and was ordained as a priest of the Roman Catholic Church in 1977. He subsequently obtained a masters in philosophy in 1989 from the University of Manchester, United Kingdom, and in 1998 a Ph.D. from Heythrop College, University of London, titled "Daily Prayer: Its Origins and Its Function." Between 1989 and 2004, he lectured in liturgy and worship at Ripon College, Cuddesdon, Oxford, and was a member of the University of Oxford Faculty of Theology.

He was received into the Orthodox Church in 1996 by Metropolitan Anthony (Bloom) and served as a priest in the Russian Orthodox Diocese of Sourozh (Moscow Patriarchate). In 2000 he was tonsured as a monk at the Russian Orthodox Patriarchal Monastery in Turin, Italy, by Igumen Andrew (Wade), before moving to the United States in 2004. In the United States, he served as a priest in the Ukrainian Orthodox Church (Ecumenical Patriarchate) and was elevated by Archbishop Anthony of that diocese to the rank of Igumen in 2007. At the time of his repose at the age of 62 in November 2008, he was priest in charge of the parish of the Nativity of the Mother of God in New Britain, Connecticut, and lecturer at Yale Theological Seminary, New Haven, Connecticut.

His other works include: *Daily Prayer in Christian Spain: A Study of the Mozarabic Office* (London: SPCK, 2000), *Joyful Light* (Oxford: St Stephen's Press, 2001) and *Daily Liturgical Prayer: Origins and Theology* (Aldershot, U.K.: Ashgate Publishing, 2004)

IGOR GASLOV was born in 1975 and lives in St Petersburg, Russia. He is a graduate of the St Petersburg Theological Seminary and Academy. Currently employed as general director of a firm of land surveyors in St Petersburg, he is active as a layman in the life of the Russian Orthodox Church.

CONTENTS

INTRODUCTION

Some years ago the editor of these notes served Divine Liturgy in the chapel of an Anglican theological college (seminary) in Bristol, together with a deacon of the same diocese with whom he had not served before. One of the Anglican seminarians afterward expressed amazement that we had been able to serve so well together without any rehearsal beforehand. There was, in fact, one slight pause owing to the two of us being used to different practices when blessing the deacon to read the Gospel (see Chapter 4 on the Divine Liturgy), but otherwise we were indeed able to carry out the service together without any particular preparation other than our prayers because we were following, and had largely internalized, the same rubrics for the celebration of the Divine Liturgy.

Early liturgical books did not contain much in the way of rubrics, but by the fourteenth century a need was perceived for authoritative directions as to how to celebrate the services precisely so that the clergy could celebrate together harmoniously and the laity would not be distracted by frantic hand signals and more or less audible asides. While he was Abbot of the Great Lavra on Mount Athos, St Philotheos Kokkinos, Patriarch of Constantinople 1353–1355 and 1364–1376, codified the liturgical rubrics for Vespers, Matins, and the Liturgy in his *Diataxeis,* which became the definitive practice of both the Greek and Slav liturgical worlds until relatively modern times. A careful comparison of the *Diataxeis* of Philotheos (which were normally included in the Greek *Great Euchologion* and may also be found in Migne's *Patrologia Graeca* 154:745–66) with what follows will show that the Russian rubrical tradition (also largely observed in Ukraine and Belarus) closely reflects that fourteenth-century codification.

Variant forms that have developed in the modern Greek and Middle Eastern churches were often the result of having to adapt liturgical celebrations to the very small churches that are characteristic of the period of the *Turkokrateia*, or other similar external pressures. While no criticism is intended of places where these changes have long been accepted practice, it would seem that introducing them into modern Slavic churches is a usually mistaken attempt to get back to perceived "original practice."

Although comprehensive rubrics can only be dated back to the fourteenth century, other indications often show that the practices laid down were in fact both ancient and according to the logic of the services. A single example may suffice: In modern Greek churches, it is common for the lamp-lighting and dawn prayers at Vespers and Matins to be read before the icon of the Savior while the holy doors remain open. In Slavic practice, the doors are closed and the celebrant stands before them and not the icon. Most of these prayers were originally prayed before the royal doors, i.e., those leading from the narthex into the nave of Hagia Sofia, and were part of the ancient Constantinopolitan cathedral office (see my *Daily Liturgical Prayer* [London: Ashgate, 2004], 95ff., for further details). Praying thus before the closed doors is more in line with St Symeon of Thessaloniki's commentary in which he saw this as betokening the exclusion of sinners from the ancient paradise (*PG* 155:636).

Chapter 4 on the Divine Liturgy was circulated privately to the clergy of the diocese of Sourozh in the United Kingdom (Patriarchate of Moscow), and the incipits of prayers and other liturgical units cited in the present work are from the editions of the liturgical books published in recent years by that diocese. There are so many English versions of the Orthodox services available at the present time that a choice had to be made as to which one to use. The editor still hopes that the clergy and laity of other dioceses and jurisdictions will find this small book a useful guide.

One of the reasons why the editor was inspired to translate Gaslov's *Pravoslavnoe Bogosluzhenie*[1] and the other sources used here was their relative simplicity and lack of fuss. Clergy often delight in arcane additions to the basic simplicity of the Byzantine Orthodox liturgical tradition. Such additions do little more than confuse clergy who are not used to them and obfuscate the liturgical rites for the people who are also participants in them. Similarly, Gaslov is quite clear that there is room for a number of variant traditions, as will be apparent, most especially in the footnotes. Within the broad Philothean tradition, there is room for some variation and no support for an extreme rubricalist mentality.

The whole purpose of the directions in this book is that both clergy and people be enabled to serve together in their common acts of prayer. Simple, straightforward, and rational rubrics that have been well internalized by the clergy can allow them the space to pray and, as they pray, to also inspire in prayer those who participate in the body of the church. Our service as clergy is always both of God and of His people.

The major part of this book is a lightly edited translation of pages 3–126 of I. V. Gaslov's *Pravoslavnoe Bogosluzhenie: Prakticheskoye Rukovodstvo dlya Klirikov i Miryan* (i.e., *Orthodox Divine Service: A Practical Handbook for Clergy and Laity*) published by Satis, St Petersburg, in 1998. The appendix on the responses to the canons of Matins is also taken from Gaslov, but much of the rest of his book presumes situations that do not, for the most part, obtain in the English-speaking Orthodox world. The notes relating to concelebration when no deacon is present are drawn from *Nastolnaya Kniga Svyashchennika* (Moscow: Lestvitsa, 1998), pages 47–48 and were originally published in the journal *Handbook for Village Pastors* in the early twentieth century. Most other comments in square brackets are editorial or indicate the other sources the editor has used. The editor takes full responsibility for any mistakes in the translation and hopes that his readers will forgive him these or any other slips.

CHAPTER I

Little Vespers and the All-Night Vigil

1. TOLLING THE BELL

Toward sunset,[1] the server comes to the Rector for the signal that it is the time to ring the bell for divine service. Having received a blessing, he goes and carries out the duty of tolling the bell as laid down in the order of the Church Typikon. The toll for Little Vespers is rung on the small bell[2] and lasts as long as is takes the ringer to read Psalm 50 or the Creed three times; then, after a short pause, he rings a little chime with the small bell and the chiming bells.

2. THE NINTH HOUR

When it is time for the reading of the Ninth Hour, the priest serving comes to church[3] and vests in a stole.[4] Having vested, the priest stands in the narthex (if the Ninth Hour is being read there), or on the ambo before the holy doors (if the Ninth Hour is served in the church)[5] and pronounces the initial exclamation: *Blessed is our God, always now and ever, and to the ages of ages.*[6]

3. THE NORMAL BEGINNING

The reader begins the order for the reading of the Ninth Hour by answering *Amen.* He then says the prayers of the Normal Beginning: *Glory to Thee, O Lord..., O heavenly King*[7]..., *Holy God..., Glory..., Both now..., All-holy*

I

Trinity..., Lord have mercy (three times), *Glory..., Both now..., Our Father....* The priest pronounces the usual exclamation: *For Thine is the kingdom....*[8] The reader answers: *Amen.* He continues to read the Ninth Hour with *Lord have mercy* (twelve times), *Glory, now and ever. O come let us worship...,* and Psalms 83, 84, and 85. *Glory..., now and ever. Alleluia* (three times).[9] *Lord have mercy* (three times). *Glory....* The troparion appointed for the day (or of the feast or saint).[10] *Both now...,* the Theotokion of the hour: *Thou Who for our sake...,* the verse of the hour: *Forsake us not utterly...,* and the Trisagion Prayers.[11]

4. The priest pronounces the usual exclamation: *For Thine is the kingdom....* The reader: *Amen* and the kontakion appointed for the day. *Lord have mercy* (forty times). *Thou Who at all times....Lord have mercy* (three times). *Glory, Both now and ever. More honorable....In the name of the Lord, father, give the blessing.* The priest responds: *God be merciful to us and bless us....* The reader says *Amen* and reads the Prayer of the Ninth Hour: *O Sovereign, Lord Jesus Christ our God....*

5. If the service is celebrated in the narthex, then the Lesser Dismissal is now given. The priest: *Glory to Thee, O Christ our God and our Hope, glory to Thee.* The people (choir): *Glory..., Both now. Lord have mercy* (three times). *Give the blessing.* And the priest says the dismissal: *May Christ our true God, through the prayers of His most pure Mother, of our venerable and God-loving fathers and all the saints, have mercy and save us, for He is good and loves mankind.* The people answer this by singing *Lord have mercy* three times, and all (priest, reader, choir, brethren, and laity) leave the narthex and enter the church, where Little Vespers is begun.

6. If the service of the Ninth Hour is held in the church, then the dismissal is omitted and Little Vespers is begun immediately after the Prayer of the Ninth Hour.

7. LITTLE VESPERS

The priest, standing before the holy doors,[12] begins by saying: *Blessed is our God, always, now and ever and to the ages of ages.* The reader: *Amen.*[13] *O come let us worship...*, and he reads Psalm 103 (the evening psalm) *Bless the Lord, O my soul...* in a quiet and tender voice. After the psalm: *Glory..., Both now..., Alleluia* (three times), *Lord have mercy* (three times).[14] *Glory..., Both now...*, and immediately they sing[15] *Lord I have cried* in the tone of the Sunday. The first choir sings the verse: *Lord, I have cried* (as at Great Vespers), the second choir *Let my prayer....*[16] The ensuing verses of Psalms 140, 141, and 129 are omitted. Having sung the verse *From the morning watch...*, the first sticheron from the Octoechos[17] is sung by the first choir. The second choir sings *For with the Lord there is mercy...* and the second sticheron. The first choir sings *Praise the lord all ye nations...* and the third sticheron. The second choir sings *For mighty is his merciful kindness...* and the fourth sticheron. Then is sung *Glory..., Both now...*, and the so-called Lesser Theotokion,[18] a sticheron in honor of the Mother of God, which is found in the order of Little Vespers in the Octoechos, immediately after which[19] the reader reads: *O Jesus Christ, Thou gentle light...*, after which the priest and the choir sing the prokeimenon.

8. The evening prokeimenon *The Lord is King* is proclaimed by the priest, two and a half times (and not four and a half as at Great Vespers). The priest: *Let us attend. Peace be with you all* (at these words, turning toward the people, the priest blesses them). *Wisdom! Let us attend. Prokeimenon in the sixth tone: The Lord is King, and has put on glorious apparel.* The first choir sings in the sixth tone: *The Lord is King....* The priest, the verse: *The Lord has put on His apparel: and girded Himself with strength.* The second choir sings: *The Lord is King...* in the same tone. The priest sings

the first half of the prokeimenon: *The Lord is King.* The first choir completes the second half of the prokeimenon: *And has put on glorious apparel.*

9. Immediately after the prokeimenon, the reader begins *Vouchsafe, O Lord...* and after this are sung the Aposticha.

10. The Aposticha are found in the Octoechos, in the order for Little Vespers of the Sunday in the appointed tone. The first choir begins to sing the first resurrection sticheron.[20] Then the second choir sings the verse: *The memory of His name is from age to age*[21] and the first verse of the stichera to the Mother of God of the Octoechos. The first choir sings the verse: *Hearken O daughter...* and the second verse to the Mother of God. The second choir sings the verse: *Thy face...* and the third verse to the Mother of God. The first choir:[22] *Glory..., Both now...,* and the Theotokion for Little Vespers in the Octoechos (of the Aposticha). Immediately after this has been sung, the reader begins: *Lord, now lettest Thou Thy servant depart in peace...* and the Trisagion Prayers. The priest, the normal exclamation: *For Thine is the kingdom....* The first choir sings *Amen* and the Resurrection Troparion, the second choir: *Glory..., Both now...,* and the Theotokion of the Resurrection Troparion.

11. Then the priest, on the ambo, pronounces the Lesser (shortened) Litany of Fervent Supplication, which has just four petitions.

Priest: *Have mercy on us....* People: *Lord, have mercy* (three times). Priest: *Again we pray for his holiness....* People: *Lord, have mercy* (three times). Priest: *Again we pray for this country....* People: *Lord, have mercy* (three times). Priest: *Again we pray for all the brethren and all Christians....* People: *Lord, have mercy* (three times). And the priest the exclamation: *For Thou, O God, art merciful....* People: *Amen.*

12. And immediately Little Vespers is closed with the Lesser Dismissal. Priest: *Glory to Thee....* People:

Glory..., Both now..., Lord, have mercy (three times), *Give the blessing.*

The priest pronounces the dismissal in the same way as at the Hours, Compline, and the Midnight Office:[23] *May Christ our true God, through the prayers of His most pure mother...* and the choir sing the Many Years: *To our great Lord and Father....*

13. In monasteries, the evening meal is served after the dismissal of Little Vespers and the Many Years, with the appointed order of prayers.

ALL-NIGHT VIGIL

14. TOLLING THE BELL

As with all divine services in the church, the All-Night Vigil begins with the ringing of the bells. "Not long after the setting of the sun" (Typikon, Chapter 2),[24] having sought and obtained from the Rector of the church the required blessing, the ringer begins the *blagovest* (single toll) and then the *trezvon* (chime), by which means the faithful are called to prayer. The *blagovest* before the beginning of the All-Night Vigil for Sunday is made on the Sunday bell (see above) and is accompanied by the recitation of the seventeenth kathisma, *Blessed are the blameless,*[25] or a reading of Psalm 50 twelve times, that will last for half an hour. Then, after a short pause, the *trezvon* is rung on all the bells, excluding only the largest, the so-called "festal" bell.

15. THE VESTING OF THE CLERGY

At the appropriate hour, the clergy go to the church for the evening service. Making three bows from the waist,[26] they enter the sanctuary through the south door and bow down three times before the altar, and begin vesting. The priest takes the stole and the deacon the stikharion (*podriznik*), and they make three bows toward the high place saying (quietly): *O God, cleanse me, a sinner, and have mercy on me*, repeating these words at each bow. Then the deacon, holding the stikharion in his right hand with the stole, comes to the priest and, bowing his head, says to him: *Bless Master, the robe and the stole.* The priest blesses, saying: *Blessed be our God....* The deacon answers *Amen*, and kissing the cross on the stikharion and the hand that gave the blessing, moves away from the priest and puts on the stikharion. Then, taking the stole and kissing the cross on it, he places it on his left shoulder. Furthermore, taking the cuffs and also kissing the cross on them, he puts them on over his hands.

16. The priest, having bowed to the high place, takes the stole with the left hand and blesses it, saying: *Blessed be our God...,* and, kissing the cross on the stole, puts it on. Then, blessing and kissing the crosses on them, the priest vests in the cuffs and phelonion.

Having vested, the deacon takes the covering off the altar. Then the priest and the deacon stand before the holy altar and make three bows with the words: *God, cleanse me a sinner and have mercy upon me,* and they kiss the edge of the altar. When the clergy reverence the altar, the server takes the already lit censer, gives it to the deacon, and the deacon gives it to the priest. Placing incense in the censer, the priest blesses the censer,[27] quietly saying the prayer of the censer: *We offer Thee incense....* The deacon now opens the curtain and the holy doors. Taking the lit deacon's candle from the server, and holding it in his left hand while holding the stole in his right, he stands at the altar, opposite the priest, and they begin the censing. Although the Typikon orders the practice of censing "crosswise,"[28] now it is simply a three-fold incensation.[29] It should be mentioned that when the deacon gives the censer to the priest and when the priest gives the censer back to the deacon, the latter always kisses the priest's hand.[30] Thus, prayerfully following this order, the priest and deacon, in silence, begin the censing of the holy sanctuary.

17. CENSING THE SANCTUARY

Beginning by censing the altar, the priest stands before the altar (i.e., at the west side) and bowing, censes it three times, the deacon standing opposite the priest holding the candle (on the east side of the altar, i.e., between the seven-branched lamp stand and the high place). As the priest bows, the deacon responds each time by also bowing from the waist. The priest then goes to the south side of the table and the deacon to the north side, and the altar is again censed three times with bows. The priest censes the altar in exactly the same way from the east side (the deacon going to the west side of the table) and then from the north side (the deacon standing at the south side of the altar). Then the priest censes the altar cross and icon and the high place (and any icon located there). After this, the priest stands before the holy preparation table, and, as the deacon stands to the south of the preparation table, he censes it. All this censing is done in strokes of three. Moving to the high place, the priest begins censing the icons in the sanctuary. From the high place, he censes the icons on the west wall of the sanctuary, beginning with the icon above the holy doors, and then if there are such, the icons on the west wall to the south of the holy doors and then those to the north. After that, moving to the south part of the sanctuary, he incenses the icons that are there, i.e., on the south wall of the sanctuary. Then, moving through the high place to the north part of the sanctuary, he incenses the icons on the north sanctuary wall. After this, the priest and deacon again move to the high place and, standing there, cense the assisting clergy, first in the south part of the sanctuary, and then the north. If the Rector of the church is presiding at the vigil but a junior priest is carrying out the censing, then before he censes the clergy in the south part of the sanctuary, he first censes the Rector. Each of the assisting clergy responds to the censing with a bow from the waist.

18. THE OPENING EXCLAMATION OF GREAT VESPERS

After the censing, the deacon, with the candle, goes out of the holy doors onto the solea, and the priest now stands before the holy altar with the censer in his hand. On the solea, looking toward the worshippers in the church (i.e., facing west), the deacon calls out in a loud voice *Arise!* and then, turning to face the altar: *Master, give the blessing.*[31] The priest makes a sign of the cross before the holy altar with the censer, exclaiming: *Glory to the holy, consubstantial....*

19. At the words: *Glory to the holy,* he lifts the censer up. At the word *consubstantial,* he lowers it. At *lifegiving,* he moves it to the right (his left), and at the words *and undivided Trinity* to the left (the priest's right). At the words: *always, now and for ever, and to the ages of ages,* the priest censes the holy table three times. The deacon, meanwhile, returns to the sanctuary and stands behind the holy altar facing the priest. The people (choir)[32] respond to the priest's exclamation: *Amen.*

20. The priest and the deacon, and also all the assisting clergy standing within the sanctuary, begin to sing, as the priest censes before the altar: *O come, let us worship God our King,* as required by the Typikon, in a low voice: *O come, let us worship and fall down before Christ, our King and our God;* a bit louder: *O come, let us worship and fall down before Christ Himself, our King and our God* in a loud voice; and then in a special way: *O come, let us worship and fall down before Him.*

21. THE INTRODUCTORY PSALM

The first choir immediately begins to sing the introductory psalm, Psalm 103,[33] starting: *Bless the Lord, O my soul* and the response: *Blessed art Thou, O Lord.* The second choir: *Bless the Lord, O my soul. O Lord my God, Thou art exceeding great,* and the response: *Blessed art Thou, O Lord.* The first choir, the verse: *Thou coverest Thyself with light as with a garment,* and the response: *Blessed art Thou, O Lord.* The second choir, the verse: *He makes His angels spirits: and His ministers a flame of fire,* and the second response: *Wonderful are thy works, O Lord.* The first choir, the verse: *The waters stand on the hills,* and the response: *Wonderful are Thy works, O Lord.* The second choir, the verse: *The waters run among the hills,* and the response: *Wonderful....* The first choir, the verse: *In wisdom hast Thou made them all,* and the response: *May the glory of the Lord endure for ever.*[34]

22. THE CENSING OF THE CHURCH

During the singing of the opening psalm, the priest with the censer and the deacon with the lit candle go out of the sanctuary and make a full censing of the church. To begin, the deacon goes to the solea, before the holy doors, while the priest, facing the doors as he also goes out of the sanctuary, censes the south leaf of the doors. Then he censes the other. Each time he censes, he and the deacon bow. Then the priest goes out onto the solea and, preceded by the deacon, begins to cense[35] the iconostasis, the klirosy, the people, and the whole church. He begins, standing on the solea before the holy doors, and censes them, and then the icons that are above them. He then censes the icon of the Savior, of the saint of the church, and of the ones that follow, i.e., all on the right side of the iconostasis. Returning to the holy doors, he censes the icon of the Mother of God, and the neighboring icons, i.e., those on the left side of the iconostasis. All this is done turned to the east, toward the altar. Now turning around before the holy doors, he censes the right kliros and those in the choir there,[36] turning around with his face toward the west, toward the people, he censes the left kliros, and then, turning again toward the people, he censes them (from the south to the west, and from the west to the north). The priest and the deacon then descend to the icon of the feast (lying on an analoy in the center of the church); it is censed three times, and, beginning from the right kliros and going around the church to his left, the priest censes the icons on the walls (and on the pillars) of the church, and also the people present, who respond as they are reverenced with a bow (he also censes those in the narthex).

23. Having thus completed the censing of the whole church, the priest and deacon return to the solea, where the priest again censes the holy doors, the icon of the Savior (on the right side) and the icon of the Mother of God (on the left side), goes through the holy doors into the sanctuary and censes before the altar, while the deacon stands near the priest[37] (to his right). Censing the deacon, the priest gives him the censer. The deacon censes the priest and bows toward the high place; he then gives the censer and the candle to the server and closes the holy doors, and the priest (on the west side) and the deacon (on the south side) take up their position before the holy table and bow before it.

24. After this, the priest, on the solea before the holy doors, must read the lamp-lighting prayers.[38] If, however, he cannot complete this before the choir has finished singing, then the priest should say these prayers in the sanctuary, during or after the Great Litany, or during the singing of the stichera on *Lord, I have cried*, so that they are all said as part of the service. But according to the rule, the greater part of the prayers should be fulfilled during the verses of Psalm 103[39] and, so long as the chant is carried out "unhurriedly and harmoniously," that will give the priest time after the censing, to read the lamp-lighting prayers before the holy doors.[40]

25. The singers finish singing Psalm 103 antiphonally or by both choirs singing *Glory..., Both now..., Alleluia, Glory be to Thee O God* (three times). The deacon then bows to the high place and to the Rector, and, going around the north side of the altar, he goes out of the north door onto the solea to take the Great Litany.[41] Standing on the solea, he makes three bows toward the sanctuary, and if the priest is still standing on the solea reading the lamp-lighting prayers, he bows to the priest, and the priest responds by bowing to him.[42]

[*It should be noted that if Great Vespers is not served as part of an All-Night Vigil, then the priest begins:* Blessed is our God... *and the reader reads the normal beginning and Psalm 103. In this case, there is no censing at this point.*]

26. THE GREAT LITANY

Holding the stole with three fingers of the right hand,[43] the deacon begins the Great Litany. The Great Litany is pronounced facing toward the sanctuary, and at each petition the deacon makes the sign of the cross and bows from the waist. Deacon: *In peace, let us pray to the Lord... and our whole life unto Christ our God.* The priest pronounces the exclamation from the sanctuary: *For to Thee belongs....* People: *Amen.* During this exclamation, the deacon returns to the sanctuary by the south door.[44] He kisses the altar at the south side (making a reverence as he does so), bows to the celebrating priest and stands in his own place, awaiting the time for the Short Litany.

[*If a priest serves without a deacon, he remains on the solea after reading the lamp-lighting prayers and takes the* Great Litany *before the holy doors.*[45]]

27. THE VESPERS KATHISMA

After the *Amen*, the choirs begin to sing the first antiphon of the first kathisma, *Blessed is the man....* According to the

Typikon, all three antiphons are sung at a Sunday Vigil,[46] and the deacon should proclaim a Small Litany after each antiphon. After the first litany, the priest says the exclamation: *For Thine is the dominion*.... After the second: *For Thou, O God, art good*..., and after the third: *For Thou art our God*.... Nowadays, only the following verses selected from the first antiphon are sung:

First choir: *Blessed is the man*..., *Alleluia* (three times),[47] Second choir: *For the Lord*....

First choir: *Serve the Lord*..., second choir: *Blessed is he*..., first choir: *Arise, O Lord*..., second choir: *The Lord is our salvation*.... The singing of the first antiphon of the first kathisma is concluded with the words: *Glory*..., *Both now*..., *Alleluia* (three times), by the choirs antiphonally, or by both together.

28. THE SMALL LITANY

After the first antiphon of the first kathisma the deacon, on the solea (in the middle of the ambo), says the Small Litany. Deacon: *Again and again*.... The priest concludes from the sanctuary: *For Thine is the dominion*.... People: *Amen.* The deacon now leaves the solea and goes back into the sanctuary.

[*A priest serving without a deacon says the Small Litany before the holy doors.*[48]]

29. THE PSALMS OF LIGHT

After the Small Litany, the singing of the Psalms of Light is begun: *Lord, I have cried,* i.e., Psalms 140, 141, 129, and 116 and the stichera in the Sunday tone from the Octoechos. According to the Typikon, these psalms are to be sung fully in the tone of the first sticheron (which at a Sunday Vigil will be the first resurrection sticheron from the Octoechos). The first choir begins:[49] *Lord, I have cried*.... Second choir: *Let my prayer be set forth*.... Then the choirs sing the remaining verses of the psalms antiphonally in a special chant, but without the response *Hear me, O Lord.*[50] First choir: *Set a watch, O Lord...,* second choir: *Incline not my heart...,* and so on in order until the verse marked "on ten," *Bring my soul out of prison....* At this point, the appointed stichera for the day are begun.

30. THE CENSING AT THE PSALMS OF LIGHT

During the singing of *Lord, I have cried,* the deacon censes the sanctuary and the church. The server gives the prepared censer to the deacon, and the deacon, putting incense into the censer and going to the north side of the altar, holds up the censer, addressing the celebrating priest: *Bless, Master, the censer.*[51] The priest blesses the censer, saying the prayer: *We offer Thee incense....* The deacon answers *Amen* and commences the censing.[52] He censes the holy altar (as was described earlier, three times with a single bow) from the west, from the south, from the east, and from the north, he then censes the cross and image on the altar, the high place, the table of preparation, and after that from the high place, the icons above the holy doors and on the west wall of the sanctuary, and after that the icons in the south part of the sanctuary, and then the north. He continues by censing the Rector and the clergy on the right side and then those on the left and goes out onto the solea by the north door. On the solea, he censes the holy doors, the icons on the right side of the iconostasis, the icons on the left side, the right kliros, the left kliros, and the people (from left to right). He then descends to the festal icon (in the middle of the church), censes it, and begins to cense the whole church, going around the perimeter, starting with the icons at the right kliros and going through the right (south) part of the church and its worshippers who are there, then censing the narthex, followed by the left (north) side of the church and the worshippers, completing the censing of the church with the icons on the left kliros. On going back to the solea, he censes the holy doors, the icon of the Savior, the icon of the Mother of God and, holding the censer in his left hand and making a sign of the cross, goes through the south door into the sanctuary. In the sanctuary, he censes the altar from the west side, then the celebrating priest (or the Rector) and, bowing to the high place, gives the censer to the server. He bows and kisses the edge of the altar, from the south side, and stands at the altar to await the Entrance of Vespers.

[*In sobors and parish churches, a priest wears the stole and chasuble for the whole service, including this censing when he serves without a deacon. The regulations for monastics are different.*[53]]

31. THE STICHERA ON THE PSALMS OF LIGHT

The singing of the stichera on *Lord, I have cried* is done in the following manner.

The canonarch, without calling out the tone because it was called at the beginning of the psalm itself: *Bring my soul out of prison*,[54] First choir: *That I may confess Thy Name*[55] and the first resurrection sticheron[56] (from the Octoechos). The canonarch: *The righteous await me.* Second choir: *Until Thou requite me* and the second resurrection sticheron. Canonarch: *Out of the depths have I cried unto Thee, O Lord.* First choir: *Lord, hear my voice* and the third resurrection sticheron. Canonarch: *Let Thine ears be attentive.* Second choir: *To the voice of my prayer* and the first of the resurrection stichera of Anatolius from the Octoechos. Canonarch: *If Thou, Lord, shouldst mark our iniquities, O Lord, who should stand.* First choir: *But there is forgiveness with Thee* and the second sticheron of Anatolius. Canonarch: *For Thy name's sake I wait upon Thee, O Lord; my soul waits upon Thy word.* Second choir: *My soul hopes in the Lord* and the third sticheron of Anatolius. Canonarch: *From the morning watch until the night, from the morning watch.* First choir: *Let Israel trust in the Lord* and the fourth sticheron of Anatolius.

32. They then begin to sing the stichera from the Menaion, of the saint or feast of that day[57] or, if they are indicated, the stichera of the Mother of God, composed by Paul of Armorium from the Octoechos. Canonarch: *In* such and such *tone* (or *in the same tone, podoben*). *For with the Lord there is mercy, and with Him is plenteous redemption.* Second choir: *And He shall redeem Israel from all his iniquities* and the first sticheron. Canonarch: *Praise the Lord, all ye nations.* First choir: *O praise Him, all ye peoples* and the second sticheron. (The following verses and stichera are to be sung together according to the Typikon, but nowadays they are distributed between both choirs.)

Canonarch: *For mighty is His merciful kindness toward us.* Second choir: *And the truth of the Lord endures for ever* and the third sticheron.

33. If the Menaion supplies a sticheron of the saint on *Glory…* then the canonarch: *Glory be, in* such and such *tone* and the first choir: *Glory to the Father, and to the Son, and to the Holy Spirit* and the sticheron "on Glory." If there is no sticheron "on Glory," then immediately the canonarch: *Glory… Holy Spirit. Both now and for ever in* such and such *tone.* First choir: *Both now and for ever, and to the ages of ages. Amen,* and they sing the Theotokion (sticheron to the Mother of God) from the Octoechos in the tone of the week. When there is a sticheron "on Glory" completed by the first choir, then the canonarch: *Both now and for ever, in* such and such *tone.* Second choir: *Both now and for ever… Amen.* And the Theotokion in the tone of the week.

34. ENTRANCE WITH THE CENSER

At the singing of the Theotokion, the holy doors are opened and the Entrance takes place. The server gives the deacon the smoking censer. The deacon takes it from the right (south) side and offers it to the priest for a blessing, saying: *Bless, Master, the censer.* The priest blesses, saying the prayer: *We offer Thee incense....* Having taken the blessing, the deacon kisses the altar at the same time as the priest and goes ahead of him around the altar, to the north door. They are preceded out by two candle bearers[58] with lit candles. The priest goes "simply," with hands lowered, behind the deacon. Thus they go out onto the solea. The candle bearers stand, the first in front of the icon of the Savior and the second in front of that of the Mother of God.[59] The priest stands before the holy doors on the solea, and the deacon incenses the holy doors, the icon of the Savior and that of the Mother of God, and the priest. He then stands a little to the right of the priest, halfway between him and the doors. Taking the censer in his left hand, and with three fingers of the right hand holding the stole, bowing a little, he says quietly, but not so as to be inaudible to the priest: *Let us pray to the Lord.* The priest reads quietly the Prayer of the Entrance: *In the evening, in the morning and noonday....*[60] Then the deacon standing before him and directing him to the east with his stole says to the priest (again quietly): *Bless, Master, the holy Entrance.* The priest blesses with a sign of the cross toward the east, saying (quietly): *Blessed is the Entrance....* The deacon quietly answers *Amen* and, taking the censer in his right hand again, and going a little to one side, he censes the priest and the choirs, and standing in his former place, waits for the singing of the sticheron to finish. When the Theotokion is finished, the deacon comes to the center of the holy doors, faces toward the altar, and making a sign of the cross with the censer, exclaims: *Wisdom! Stand aright.*

35. EVENING HYMN OF LIGHT

The choir begins to sing: *O Jesus Christ, Thou gentle light*... and the deacon goes into the sanctuary, censing the altar from its four sides, and then the holy place (and the Rector[61]) and gives the censer to the server. The priest, having made a reverence in the direction of the altar, kisses the icons on the holy doors. The candle bearers meanwhile stand on the solea before the holy doors holding their candles. Having kissed the icons, the priest turns and blesses the candle bearers, who respond with a bow and carry their candles into the sanctuary.[62] Having blessed the candle bearers, the priest enters the sanctuary and, at the same time as the deacon (who is standing to his right), makes a bow and kisses the edge of the altar. Then the priest and deacon go to the high place, making a reverence toward it and standing behind the altar, the priest opposite the southeast corner of the table, and the deacon to the north of the priest, facing the people. At the end of the hymn, the evening prokeimenon is sung.

36. THE EVENING PROKEIMENON

The priest and deacon stand near the high place, facing west. The deacon: *Let us attend;* the priest, blessing the people: *Peace be with you all.* The deacon: *Wisdom! Let us attend. Prokeimenon in the sixth tone: The Lord is King, and has put on glorious apparel.* The first choir repeats the prokeimenon. The deacon: *The Lord has put on...,* and the second choir: Prokeimenon. Deacon: *He has made the round world...,* and the first choir: Prokeimenon. Deacon: *Holiness becomes...,* and the second choir: Prokeimenon. The deacon, the first half of the prokeimenon: *The Lord is King.* The first choir completes the prokeimenon: *And has put on glorious apparel.* During the singing of the prokeimenon, the priest stands near the high place, facing the people, his hands by his sides.

37. LITANY OF FERVENT SUPPLICATION

At the end of the prokeimenon, the priest and deacon bow to the high place and to each other, and then the priest goes to stand before the altar, while the deacon closes the holy doors, bows to the altar, and kisses the edge of it from the north side and then goes out through the north door onto the solea for the Litany of Fervent Supplication. If the church possesses an ambo, then he pronounces the litany from there. Deacon: *Let us all say....* At the end, the priest, at the altar, says the exclamation: *For Thou, O God, art merciful....* The people: *Amen.* The deacon goes back into the sanctuary by the south door, bowing toward the altar.

[*When the priest serves without a deacon, then, as at weekday Vespers, this litany should be taken before the holy doors[63] "For the better hearing of the worshippers."[64]*]

38. EVENING PRAYER

After the litany comes the prayer *Vouchsafe, O Lord to keep us this evening without sin....* The modern Typikon of the Russian church expects this prayer to be read by the reader (or the Rector), and the same should be done at All-Night Vigil as is done at daily Vespers. In many Russian churches today, however, it is normal for this prayer to be sung by the people or even by those within the sanctuary. This practice does not contradict the Church Typikon and, it is agreed, is even referred to in old notes of the Jerusalem Typikon as accepted now in Russia.

39. EVENING LITANY

After the prayer *Vouchsafe,* the deacon, making the normal bow, goes out to the solea by the north door for the Evening Litany. This litany is said not on the ambo but on the solea, before the holy doors. Deacon: *Let us complete....* At the end, the priest at the altar exclaims: *For Thou, O God, art merciful....* People: *Amen.* During this exclamation, the deacon stands before the icon of the Savior.

40. The priest, turning round to face to the west, gives aloud a blessing to the worshippers in the church: *Peace be with you all.* People: *And with thy spirit.* The deacon, lifting up his stole as in a litany: *Let us bow our heads to the Lord.* All the worshippers bow their heads (without making a sign of the cross) and reply in a protracted way: *To Thee, O Lord.* The priest before the altar quietly reads the prayer at the bowing of heads: *O Lord our God, Who didst bow the heavens...* and after it exclaims aloud: *Blessed and glorified be the might....* People: *Amen.*

[*If the priest serves without a deacon, this litany and the prayer of inclination are taken before the holy doors; he returns to the sanctuary during the Aposticha.*[65]]

41. And they begin to sing the stichera of the Lity. If there is no Lity appointed on this day or if it is normal for the Lity to be omitted, then in place of the stichera of the Lity, they immediately begin to sing the Aposticha.

42. THE LITY

The deacon reenters the sanctuary by the south door during the exclamation *Blessed and glorified be the might,* and the choirs begin to sing antiphonally the stichera of the Lity. On festal vigils, the stichera for the Lity will be found in the services of the feast; on Sunday vigil Lity, the stichera of the church are sung, i.e., the Lity stichera of the service for the dedication of the church (be that of a feast, icon, or saint); this can be done by the canonarch and is without verses. One may sing the sticheron of the church in the *samoglasen* melodies, which are the most beautiful way of executing this chant. After the stichera (or sticheron), the Lity is completed by *Glory..., Both now...,* and the sticheron of the Mother of God from the first supplement to the Menaion (i.e., the Theotokia stichera of the resurrection) "from the verses." If the church is dedicated to Christ or the Mother of God, then, after completing the verses of the church, on *Glory..., Both now...* is sung the sticheron of the feast (i.e., from the service of the dedicatory festival).

43. During the singing of the Lity verses, the priest and the deacon go from the sanctuary to the narthex of the church, where, at the same time, the worshippers in the church should also go.

44. The Typikon is clear that this procession is done in a manner similar to that of the Vespers Entrance. The deacon takes the censer from the server and presents it to the priest for a blessing in the normal manner. Then the priest in stole and cuffs, and skufia or kamilavkion, makes a reverence to the altar together with the deacon. They go out, going around the altar, out of the north door, preceded by two candle bearers to the narthex, where the deacon censes the icons that are there, the priest, the brethren, and those standing there about the priest, from a little to the right of him. The holy doors remain closed throughout all this.[66]

45. In actual common practice, the procession at the Lity is carried out in a somewhat different manner. The holy doors are opened. Before them on the solea stand the two candle bearers with their lit candles, having gone out, one through the south and one through the north door. The priest, in phelonion, stole, and cuffs and wearing skufia or kamilavkion, blesses the censer held by the deacon; together they reverence the altar, and going out of the holy doors the priest goes to the narthex of the church. He is preceded by the two candle bearers. On arrival in the narthex,[67] they stand in the following order: in front (i.e., to the east), the two candle bearers;[68] behind them (i.e., to the west), in the middle of the narthex, the priest facing the altar. In the meantime, the deacon makes a normal censing of the altar, the sanctuary,

the iconostasis, the whole church, and the holy doors and then goes to the narthex to the priest, standing before him, a little to his right,[69] and gives the censer to the server.

46. Then follow the prayers of the Lity. Deacon: *O God, save Thy people*.... All, as in the *Sluzhebnik* to the end of the priest's exclamation: *Hear us O God our Savior.* The priest, turning toward the west, then blesses the worshippers: *Peace be with you all.* People: *And with thy spirit.* Deacon: *Let us bow*.... All the worshippers bow their head without making a sign of the cross. People: *To Thee, O Lord.* The priest facing toward the sanctuary[70] reads aloud the prayer: *Most Merciful Master*... and the people sing *Amen,* which finishes the Lity.

47. APOSTICHA

The choirs begin to sing the Aposticha antiphonally;[71] the first sticheron is sung directly without any introductory verse. Canonarch: *In* such and such *tone* and the first line of the first sticheron. First choir sings the first resurrection sticheron (from the Octoechos)

Canonarch: *The Lord reigns.* Second choir: *He is clothed in majesty* and the second resurrection sticheron. Canonarch: *For he has established the world*.... First choir: *And it shall not be moved* and the third sticheron. Canonarch: *Holiness befits Your house Lord.* Second choir: *For length of days*... and the fourth sticheron. If there is a sticheron of the saint on "Glory," then canonarch: *Glory, in tone* so and so. First choir: *Glory*... *Spirit* and the sticheron on "Glory" from the Menaion. Canonarch: *Now and ever, in the same tone.* Second choir: *Both now*... and the Theotokion of the resurrection Aposticha, in the tone of the *Glory* of the saint, from the first appendix of the Menaion. If there is no sticheron of the saint on "Glory," then canonarch: *Glory to the Father and the Son and to the Holy Spirit, Both now and ever* in the same tone. First choir: *Both now . . .* and the Theotokion Apostichon from the Octoechos, in the tone of the Sunday.

48. During the singing of the Aposticha, the candle bearers take up their candlesticks with lighted candles and, preceding the clergy, go back through the church. In the middle of the church, opposite the holy doors, the server places a table with the Lity tray upon it, removing the covers that keep the vessels decent for the blessing of the five loaves, the wheat, and the two small containers, one to the left (of the worshippers) for wine, the other to the right for oil. On both sides (somewhat to the back) of the Lity vessels, the Lity candlesticks should stand. The clergy stand before the Lity table, the deacon a little to the right of the priest. The candle bearers place their candlesticks on either side of the icon of the feast (if it is in the middle of the church; if not, they place the candlesticks on either side of the Lity table), and they then stand a little way back, facing one another. Then all wait for the singing of the troparion *Mother of God and Virgin . . . .*

49. The Song of Simeon and the Trisagion Prayers

After the singing of the Aposticha, it is expected that the Rector will read the prayer: *Lord, now lettest Thou Thy servant depart. . . .* Nowadays, this prayer is sung by one of the choirs; this does not contradict the oldest directions of the Jerusalem Typikon. The reader then reads the Trisagion Prayers. During this, the server gives the censer to the deacon, who places incense in it and holds it up before the priest for a blessing.

50. The Dismissal Troparion of Vespers

The reader finishes the *Our Father* and the priest pronounces the normal exclamation: *For Thine is the kingdom . . . .* The people sing *Amen* and begin to sing three times the troparion *Mother of God and Virgin* ... in the fourth tone (antiphonally if there are two choirs).

[NB: *If Great Vespers is not served as part of an All-Night Vigil, then* Mother of God and Virgin *and Psalm 33 are not sung, but the Dismissal Troparia for the day are sung, followed by the normal conclusion as at paragraphs 97 and 98.*]

51. THE BLESSING OF THE FIVE LOAVES

During the singing of the troparion, the deacon censes the table in this order: While the troparion is sung three times, he censes around the four sides of the table. Then he censes the table from the middle[72] and, with a bow, censes the priest (or the Rector). The priest responds by bowing in return, and the deacon gives the censer to the server. Then, after the third singing of the troparion, the deacon exclaims: *Let us pray to the Lord.*

The people respond: *Lord, have mercy.* The priest now takes one of the loaves (the uppermost) and with it makes a sign of the cross over the other loaves, and then, kissing this loaf, although it is not yet blessed, places it back on top of the other four. He then reads aloud the Prayer of the Blessing of the Five Loaves: *O Lord Jesus Christ, our God....* At the word "bless," the priest does as he says and blesses the named objects;[73] at the words "these loaves," with the hand over the loaves; "wheat," lowering the hand over the wheat; "wine," over the vessel with the wine to the priest's left; "and oil," over the vessel with the oil in it to the right, so that he makes a sign of the cross over them.

52. PSALM 33

After the blessing of the loaves, the choir sings: *Amen. Blessed be the Name of the Lord* ... (three times) and the first half of Psalm 33: *I will bless the Lord at all times....*[74] During the singing of Psalm 33, the priest goes onto the solea and, standing before the holy doors,[75] faces the west (but in some places faces east) to await the end of the singing of Psalm 33. The deacon meanwhile (or the server) carries the objects that have been blessed through the north door into the sanctuary. At the end of Psalm 33, the priest, facing west (if he has waited for the ending looking toward the east, then he turns around to his right), blesses the people with the words: *The blessing of the Lord be upon you...* and goes into the sanctuary through the holy doors,[76] after which the holy doors are closed. The people sing: *Amen* and having now finished Vespers, Matins begins. After the priest and deacon have gone into the sanctuary, they make reverent bows, kissing the edge of the altar.

SUNDAY MATINS

53. THE TOLLING OF THE BELL FOR MATINS

Before the beginning of Matins (or as the service begins), the ringer tolls the bell. In one tradition, this is a double ring, though not for long; in another (called here the chime, and done in the same way as at the beginning of daily Matins), it is a single deliberate tolling that might last the time it would take to read through Psalm 50. The Typikon for the All-Night Vigil remarks only that it is done with the great bell and other bells.

[*When Matins is not served as part of an All-Night Vigil, then it begins with the "Royal Beginning" and the censing during that, for which see the rubrics, for example, in the* Sluzhebnik, Vespers and Matins *(Oxford: St Stephen's Press, 2001), 41–45.*]

54. THE SIX PSALMS

In the order of the All-Night Vigil, Matins begins immediately after *Amen,* with the reading of the Six Psalms.

The Typikon is clear that the Six Psalms are read by the Rector. Nowadays, though, in parish churches where the Rector is usually also the celebrating priest, the Six Psalms are read by the reader, standing below the solea in front of the holy doors, in a quiet but audible voice, with all due attention, not carelessly but in the fear of God, as if the unseen God Himself were speaking. "The brethren listen with attention; because these psalms sum up repentance and humility, that all may know that no powers can threaten, nor overcome them: but, attending to that which is read by the reader, we stand with hands by the side, heads bowed, and eyes looking down, warm-heartedly facing east, praying about our sins, recalling death, the last torments, and life eternal."[77]

55. At the beginning are read the verses *Glory to God in the highest...* (thrice) and *O Lord Thou shalt open my lips...* (twice). Then follow Psalms 3, 37, and 62. At the end of the reading of these three psalms: *Glory..., Both now..., Alleluia* (three times). *Lord, have mercy* (three times). *Glory..., Both now...,* without bows.

56. MATINS PRAYERS

During this (i.e., *Glory...* etc.), the priest makes a reverence and kisses the altar, and goes out of the north door onto the solea. According to the Typikon, he wears only the stole, but it has come to be the practice in Russia, in non-monastic churches, for him normally to be vested in stole, cuffs, and phelonion, and with head uncovered. Having come onto the solea, he stands before the holy doors and makes a reverence, and he begins to read the twelve Matins prayers quietly.

57. The reader continues to read the next three psalms: 87, 102, and 142, and then *Glory..., Both now..., Alleluia* (three times), thus finishing the reading.

58. As the reading comes to an end, the deacon, kissing the altar, goes out of the north door onto the solea, and, at the same time as the priest, makes three reverences before the holy doors (the deacon in front of the icon of the Mother of God, the priest in front of the icon of the Savior), after which they bow to each other. Then the priest returns to the altar by the south door, kisses the altar, and stands in his normal place before it (continuing the morning prayers if he could not finish them all on the solea), and the deacon before the holy doors pronounces the Great Litany: *In peace, let us pray to the Lord* and so on. After the priest's exclamation *For to Thee belongs...*, choir: *Amen.* And then the singing of *The Lord is God* in the Sunday tone.

59. THE LORD IS GOD

The deacon, having said the Great Litany, goes before the icon of the Savior[78] and, lifting up his stole, exclaims: *The Lord is God and has appeared unto us, blessed is he that comes in the name of the Lord.* First choir in the Sunday tone: *The Lord is God....*

Deacon, the verse:[79] *O give thanks unto the Lord....* Second choir in the Sunday tone: *The Lord is God....* Deacon: *All the nations compassed me....* First choir in the Sunday tone: *The Lord is God....* Deacon: *I will not die, but live....* Second choir: *The Lord is God....*

Deacon: *The stone which the builders rejected....* First choir: *The Lord is God....*

[*If the priest is serving without a deacon, he remains on the solea for the* Great Litany *and* The Lord is God.[80]]

60. TROPARIA ON "THE LORD IS GOD"

The choirs then sing the troparia antiphonally. First they sing the Sunday Troparion twice in the appointed tone, then, on *Glory be,* the troparion of the saint from the Menaion if there is one, and then on *Both now...*, the Hymn to the Mother of God from the third appendix to the Menaion, in the same tone as the troparion on "Glory." If there is no troparion on "Glory," then after *Glory..., Both now...*, they sing the Hymn to the Mother of God of the appointed tone (i.e., that of Sunday).

61. Having finished *The Lord is God,* the deacon, during the singing of the troparia, goes into the sanctuary by the south door and bows to the altar.

62. THE KATHISMATA OF MATINS

After the singing of the troparia and Theotokion, the readings from the Psalter are begun; i.e., the appointed reading for Sunday Matins of the second and third kathismata.[81]

People: *Lord, have mercy* (three times), *Glory....* Reader: *Both now...*, second stasis of the second kathisma, then *Glory....* People: *Both now..., Alleluia* (three times), *Lord have mercy* (three times), *Glory....* Reader: *Both now...* and the third stasis of the second kathisma, then *Glory..., Both now..., Alleluia* (three times).

63. The deacon goes out of the north door onto the solea and, before the holy doors, pronounces the Small Litany, *Again and again.* The priest, the exclamation: *For Thine is the dominion....* People: *Amen.*

64. The reader reads the first Sessional Hymn from the Octoechos, the verse: *Arise, O Lord my God...* and the second Sessional Hymn, *Glory..., Both now...,* and the Theotokion.[82]

65. The third kathisma is then read in the same way as the second. After the Small Litany, the priest exclaims: *For Thou, O God, art good....* People: *Amen.* The reader reads the next set of Sessional Hymns from the Octoechos. After the first, the verse: *I will confess Thee, O Lord, with my whole heart...,* and after the second, *Glory..., Both now...,* and the Theotokion.

[*When there is no deacon, the priest says the* Small Litanies *before the holy doors, coming out by the north door and returning by the south.*[83]]

66. POLYELEOS

During the reading of the latter Sessional Hymns, the holy doors are opened. The server gives the deacon the censer, and he, in his turn, gives it to the priest. The priest places incense in the censer and blesses it. The server gives a lit candle to the deacon. The priest is to be preceded in the censing the same as at the beginning of the All-Night Vigil, censing the altar, the sanctuary, the iconostasis, the whole church, and then returning to the sanctuary.

67. While this is being done, the choir sings the Polyeleos[84] (consisting of selected verses of Psalms 134 and 135[85]): *Praise the name of the Lord..., Alleluia* (three times),[86] *Blessed is the Lord out of Sion..., Give thanks unto the Lord..., Give thanks unto the God of heaven....* Then straight away the choir sings the resurrection troparia on "Blessed is the blameless"[87] in the fifth tone: *Blessed art Thou, O Lord: teach me Thy statutes...* (the Evlogitaria).

68. In those churches where there may be a concelebrated service (i.e., a service with several priests and deacons), the censing at the Sunday service of the All-Night Vigil is carried out in the following manner. During the Sessional Hymns, the candle bearers go and stand on the solea in front of the holy doors. In the sanctuary, all the clergy vest appropriately to their rank. The deacon opens the holy doors, and the group of clergy (as would also be the case where there is only one priest and deacon) go out, preceded by the candle bearers into the middle of the church where the icon of the resurrection has been placed on an analoy. The candle bearers place their candles down beside the analoy and stand facing each other, a little distance back

from their candles.[88] The server brings the censer out of the sanctuary, and the candle for the deacon. If several priests serve together, then the servers bring candles for all the priests. The server gives the censer to the deacon, and the deacon, in his turn, to the Rector (or celebrating priest). The server gives the lit candle to the deacon (other assistants give the candles to the assisting priests). The censing is then begun.

69. The Rector (or celebrating priest) censes, with the deacon going before him. He first censes the festal icon on the analoy in the middle of the church, then around it from the four sides. Then he goes into the sanctuary and censes the altar as normal, and the whole sanctuary. Going out of the sanctuary, he censes both wings of the holy doors, then the icons on the right side of the iconostasis and then those on the left. The deacon stands by the right side of the priest, and they cense the clergy (first those on the right side of the church, then those on the left). Then the klirosy (both left and right) are incensed and the people as normal. Then they begin from the right kliros to cense the whole church and the worshippers in it. Finishing the censing at the left kliros and remounting the solea, they cense the holy doors, the icon of the Savior, and the icon of the Mother of God. They then return to the analoy with the festal icon in the middle of the church, censing it once more, then the celebrating clergy. Finally, the priest censes the deacon and gives him the censer. The deacon censes the priest and gives the censer to the server.

70. During the singing of the psalms of the Polyeleos, the ringer rings a chime on many bells, which should last until the reading of the Gospel.

71. If the censing is performed according to the first model, then the priest remains in the sanctuary, but the deacon, after the Evloghitaria, goes out to the solea and says the

Small Litany, *Again and again*.... The priest, the exclamation: *For blessed is Thy name*.... Choir: *Amen.*

72. The choir then sings[89] the Ypakoë in the tone (from the Octoechos) and the Hymn of Degrees in the appointed tone (also from the Octoechos). During the singing, the deacon returns to the sanctuary.

73. MATINS PROKEIMENON

Deacon: *Let us attend. Wisdom! The Prokeimenon in* such and such *tone* and the prokeimenon itself. The choir sings the prokeimenon, the deacon the verse, the choir the prokeimenon again; then the deacon the first half of the prokeimenon, and the choir the second half. Deacon: *Let us pray to the Lord.* People: *Lord, have mercy.* The priest exclaims: *For Thou, our God, art holy*.... People: *Amen.* Deacon: *Let everything*.... Choir: *Let everything*.... Deacon: *Praise God in His saints*.... Choir: *Let everything*....

Deacon: *Let everything that has breath.* Choir: *Praise the Lord.*

74. MATINS GOSPEL

Deacon: *And that He will count us*.... People: *Lord, have mercy* (three times). Deacon: *Wisdom! Stand aright! Let us listen to the holy Gospel.* Priest, giving a blessing to the people: *Peace be with you all.* People: *And with thy spirit.* The priest reads the introduction to the Gospel lesson: *The reading is from the holy Gospel according to* N.

75. If the censing was carried out according to the second method, then there are two ways in which the service may be continued. In the first, at the time of the Small Litany of the Polyeleos, all the clergy return to the sanctuary, where they divest and the celebrating priest alone remains vested. In the other practice, the deacon goes into the sanctuary after the Small Litany, where he picks up the holy Gospel book (kissing it as he does so), goes out of the holy doors onto the solea,

and stands on the ambo facing west. Here he pronounces the exclamations and prokeimena. Then the deacon goes with the Gospel book to the middle of the church and holds the Gospel before his chest so that the Rector (or celebrating priest) might read from it.

76. In the first method, the priest reads the Gospel in the sanctuary at the altar, facing east. When it is time for the priest to announce the title of the Gospel, the server gives a lighted candle, in a candlestick, to the deacon, and the deacon stands with it between the holy doors.

77. After the title of the holy Gospel, the people sing: *Glory to Thee, O Lord, Glory to Thee.* Deacon: *Let us attend.* And the priest reads the resurrection Gospel in the ordinary way. After the reading of the Gospel, the people sing: *Glory to Thee, O Lord, glory to Thee. We have seen the resurrection of Christ...,* and Psalm 50 is read. During this, the priest kisses the Gospel he has read[90] and closes the book, holds it before his chest, and preceded by the deacon holding the candle, goes out of the holy doors to the middle of the church, where he places the Gospel book upon a prepared analoy, the deacon standing by with his candle. Then the priest stands before the analoy with the deacon to his right. The Gospel book remains on the analoy in the middle of the church, after it has been read, for the kissing of the Gospel.

[*If there is no deacon, the priest returns to the altar after the censing and remains there for all that follows, including the reading of the Gospel (facing east). After reading the Gospel, he brings the book out to the analoy.*[91]]

78. THE KISSING OF THE GOSPEL

After the singing of *We have seen...,* the priest and those with him make two bows from the waist, kiss the Gospel, and then make another bow from the waist.[92] Such is also the order for the bowing before and venerating of the holy

Gospel by the rest of the faithful.[93] The Russian Typikon of 1641 provides a form of words to be used at the kissing of the holy Gospel, quietly by each of the faithful when they come before the Gospel book: *With fear and love I draw near to Thee, O Christ, and I believe Thy words; let fear cleanse sin, let love bring salvation.* After kissing is said quietly the following prayer: *I believe, O Lord, in Your holy gospel, O Christ God protect and save me.*

79. After the reading of Psalm 50, the people sing: *Glory..., At the prayers of the Apostles..., Both now..., At the prayers of the Mother of God..., Have mercy on me, O God...* in the sixth tone, and then the Sunday sticheron in the sixth tone: *Jesus is risen from the dead....* If there was a Lity and blessing of loaves at Vespers, then after the kissing of the Gospel, the faithful are anointed with the oil that was blessed at Vespers and also receive the blessed bread, dipped in the wine.

80. During the singing of the Sunday sticheron, the deacon, making a bow to the priest, goes up to the solea,[94] stands before the icon of the Savior, and when the singing has finished says the prayer: *O God, save thy people...* as at the Lity.[95] At the end of the prayer, he bows to the priest, and goes to the middle of the church[96] and stands in his place. The people sing: *Lord, have mercy* (twelve times).

81. THE CANON OF MATINS

The priest, aloud: *Through the mercy....* Choir: *Amen,* and they begin to sing the Canon or, to be precise, the first Eirmos of the first ode of the Canon of the Resurrection.

When the people have finished venerating the Gospel book, the priest takes it from the analoy and, preceded by the candle bearers, goes back to the sanctuary, signing the people with it at the holy doors, and placing it on the altar.

82. The Canon comprises nine odes (but the second is used only on certain days in the Great Fast). Each ode is carried out in the following manner: The choir: Eirmos of the Canon of the Resurrection. Then the reader: three troparia from the Resurrection Canon (with the response *Glory to Thy holy resurrection, O Lord*), three troparia from the Canon of the Cross and Resurrection (with the response *Glory to Thy precious cross and resurrection, O Lord*), three troparia from the Canon of the Mother of God (with the response: *Most holy Mother of God, save us*), and four troparia of the Canon of the saint from the Menaion (with the response proper to that saint).[97] Choir: the appointed Katavasia.

83. After the third ode, the deacon goes out to the solea by the north door and, standing before the holy doors, says the Small Litany: *Again and again....* The priest exclaims: *For Thou art our God....* People: *Amen.* The reader reads the Sessional Hymn of Sunday, *Glory..., Both now...,* and the Theotokion. But if appointed, he reads the kontakion and ikos of the saint from the Menaion, and then the Sessional Hymn of the saint, *Glory..., Both now...,* and the Theotokion.

84. Then the people begin to sing the Eirmos of the fourth ode. After the sixth ode, the deacon again comes before the holy doors and says the Small Litany. The priest exclaims: *For Thou art the King of peace....* People: *Amen.* Then the reader reads the kontakion and ikos of the Sunday.

[*If he serves without a deacon, the priest says the litanies after the third and sixth odes, on the solea, before the holy doors.*[98]]

85. THE CENSING AT "MORE HONORABLE"

During the eighth and ninth odes, the deacon censes the sanctuary and the whole church. The server hands the prepared censer to the deacon, the deacon places incense in it and asks the priest's blessing on the censer. Then he begins to cense the altar and the whole church in the same way as was done during the verses of *Lord I have cried*.

86. The reader, when reading the troparia of the eighth ode of the canon, replaces the response *Glory...* with *We bless the Lord, Father, Son, and Holy Spirit*. The people, before the Katavasia of the eighth ode, while making a reverence, sing: *We praise, we bless, we worship the Lord, praising and exalting Him above all for ever*. During this, the deacon comes out of the north door from the sanctuary with the censer, makes an incensation of the holy doors, the right side of the iconostasis, and stands before the icon of the Mother of God to await the end of the Katavasia.

87. At the end of the Katavasia, the deacon censes the icon of the Mother of God, exclaiming: *The Mother of God and Mother of Light, let us magnify in hymns*. He continues, censing the left side of the iconostasis, the klirosy, the people, and the whole church. Then the deacon, returning to the solea, again censes the holy doors, the icons of the Savior and the Mother of God, and returns by the south door into the sanctuary, doing there all that was noted before at *Lord, I have cried*.

88. MAGNIFICAT

After the deacon's exclamation, the choirs (antiphonally) sing in the sixth tone:[99] *My soul magnifies the Lord...* with *More honorable than the cherubim...* after each verse, and then the ninth ode of the canon. After the ninth ode, the deacon, on the solea, in front of the holy doors, exclaims the Small Litany. The priest: *For all the powers of heaven...*. People: *Amen*.

[NB: *When there is no deacon, the priest says this litany inside the sanctuary, before the altar.*[100]]

89. HOLY IS THE LORD OUR GOD

The deacon, standing before the holy doors, sings in the tone of the week: *Holy is the Lord our God.* First choir in the same tone: *Holy is the Lord our God.* Deacon: *For holy is the Lord our God.* Second choir: *Holy is the Lord our God.* Deacon: *Over all people is our God.* First choir: *Holy is the Lord our God.*

90. And the choir immediately sings[101] the Sunday Exapostilarion (according to the number of the resurrection Gospel), if there is an Exapostilarion of a saint from the Menaion: *Glory..., Both now...,* and the Theotokion of the Sunday Exapostilarion.

91. THE PRAISES (LAUDS)

The singing of the praise psalms is begun with the verses on *Praise ye.* Canonarch: *In* such and such *tone,*[102] *Let everything that has breath praise the Lord.* First choir, in the tone announced by the canonarch: *Let everything...To Thee is due praise, O God.* Second choir: *Praise Him, O all angels of His...To Thee is due praise, O God.* Then, in the same way as at *Lord I have cried,* they sing[103] the remaining verses of Psalms 148 and 149, antiphonally, the first choir beginning with *Praise Him, sun and moon....* They continue in this fashion until *To bind their kings in shackles: and their nobles with manacles of iron* inclusive.

92. THE VERSES ON THE PRAISES

The canonarch: *To pass upon them....* First choir: *This glory shall be for all His saints* and the first resurrection sticheron on the Praises. Canonarch: *Praise God in His saints.* Second choir: *Praise Him in the firm foundation of His power* and the second resurrection sticheron. Canonarch: *Praise Him for His mighty acts.* First choir: *Praise Him according to the multitude of His greatness* and the third resurrection sticheron.

Canonarch: *Praise Him with the sound of the trumpet.* Second choir: *Praise Him with psaltery and harp* and the fourth resurrection sticheron. Canonarch: *Praise Him with tambourine and dance.* First choir: *Praise Him with strings and flute* and the first sticheron of Anatolios. Canonarch: *Praise Him with well-tuned cymbals: Praise Him with loud cymbals.* Second choir: *Let everything that has breath praise the Lord* and the second sticheron of Anatolios. Canonarch, the Sunday verse: *Arise, O Lord my God, let Thy hand be lifted up.* First choir:[104] *Forget not Thy poor for ever* and the third Anatolian sticheron. Canonarch: *I will confess Thee, O Lord, with my whole heart.* Second choir: *I will speak of all Thy marvelous works* and the fourth Anatolian sticheron. Canonarch: *Glory be . . . in* such and such *tone*[105] (First choir) *Glory . . . Spirit* and the Gospel sticheron, as appointed for the Matins Gospel of that Sunday. Canonarch: *Both now and for ever,* in the second tone (second choir in the second tone[106]) *Both now . . . Amen. Most blessed art Thou. . . .*

93. At the singing of this last sticheron, the holy doors are opened. If the service is concelebrated, then the clergy are all vested from this point until the end of the Matins.

The presiding priest (or Rector) stands before the altar, vested in phelonion, and the deacon, having opened the holy doors, stands to his right. At the end of the sticheron *Most blessed art Thou,* the priest exclaims aloud: *Glory to Thee Who has shown us the light.* There is no direction for him to lift up his hands.[107]

94. THE GREAT DOXOLOGY AND THE RESURRECTION TROPARION

The choirs (together) begin to sing the Great Doxology: *Glory to God in the highest. . . .* At the end of the singing of the Trisagion, without any other exclamation being interposed, they sing the Resurrection Troparion. For the first, third, fifth, and seventh tones: *Today salvation is come into the world...,* and for the second, fourth, sixth, and eighth tones: *By rising from the tomb....*

95. THE LITANY OF FERVENT SUPPLICATION AND THE MORNING LITANY

The deacon, making a reverence to the altar and to the priest, goes out, around the altar, through the north door on to the solea and, before the holy doors, says the Litany of Fervent Supplication: *Have mercy on us, O God....* The priest exclaims: *For Thou, O God, art merciful....* People: *Amen.* The deacon continues with the Morning Litany: *Let us complete our morning prayer to the Lord,* all the petitions being the same as at Vespers except the third, *That the whole day may be perfect....* At the end, the priest exclaims: *For Thou art the God of mercy....* People: *Amen.*

96. The deacon goes before the icon of the Savior, and the priest, turning to face the west, blesses the people, exclaiming: *Peace be with you all.* People: *And with thy spirit.* The deacon: *Let us bow our heads to the Lord.* People: *To Thee, O Lord.*[108] The priest quietly reads the prayer: *O holy Lord...* and then exclaims aloud: *For Thine it is to show mercy....* People: *Amen.*

97. The deacon: *Wisdom!* People: *Give the blessing.* The priest blesses: *Blessed is He Who is, Christ our God, always, now and for ever and to the ages of ages.* During this, the deacon goes back into the sanctuary by the south door, kisses the edge of the altar, and bows to the priest. The people respond to the priest's exclamation: *Amen. Confirm, O God....*

98. THE DISMISSAL OF MATINS

The priest: *Most holy Mother of God, save us.* People: *More honor-able....* Priest: *Glory to Thee, O Christ our God and our hope, glory to Thee.* People: *Glory..., Both now..., Lord have mercy* (three times). *Give the blessing.* The priest kisses the altar, stands in the holy doors (without going out onto the solea) facing the people, i.e., to the west, and pronounces the Sunday dismissal: *May He Who is risen from the dead, Christ our true God ... for He is good and loves mankind.* The people sing the Many Years: *To our great Lord and Father....*

99. The priest goes into the sanctuary, the deacon closes the holy doors and draws the curtain across, and together they make a reverence and kiss the edge of the altar, bow to one another, leave the altar, and divest. However, the priest remains vested in stole and cuffs.

100. THE FIRST HOUR

As soon as the Many Years is finished, the reader begins the First Hour: *O come, let us worship* ... and Psalms 5, 89, and 100,[109] *Glory..., Both now..., Alleluia* (three times), *Lord, have mercy* (three times). If the feast of a saint is celebrated, the Troparion of Sunday is read first, then *Glory...* and the troparion of the saint, *Both now...* and the Theotokion of the hour *What shall we call Thee....* If there is no celebration of the feast of a saint, then *Glory...,* Troparion of Sunday, *Both now...,* and the Theotokion of the hour. The verses of the hour: *Direct my steps ... all the day long* are now read, and then the Trisagion Prayers. At the end of the *Our Father,* the priest in the sanctuary exclaims: *For Thine is the kingdom...,* and the reader says *Amen* and the kontakion of Sunday. He then says: *Lord, have mercy* (forty times) and the prayer: *Thou Who at all times..., Lord, have mercy* (three times), *Glory..., Both now..., More honorable..., In the name of the Lord, give the blessing, Father.* During this, the priest comes out on to the solea and, standing before the holy doors, says: *God be merciful to us...* and the reader answers: *Amen.* The priest turns toward the icon of the Savior and reads the prayer of the First Hour: *O Christ, the true light....* Reader: *Amen.* Then the priest turns toward the icon of the Mother of God, and the people sing the kontakion: *To Thee, O Mother of God, our leader in battle and defender...*, in the eighth tone. Priest: *Glory to Thee, O Christ our God and our hope, glory to Thee.* People: *Glory..., Both now..., Lord, have mercy* (three times), *Give the blessing.* The priest on the solea, turning to face the people, pronounces the Lesser Dismissal, beginning with the words: *May He Who is risen from the dead* and continuing: *Christ our true God....* The people respond by singing *Lord, have mercy* three times. The priest goes back into the sanctuary, where he divests. Thus is finished the order of the All-Night Vigil.

Appendix 1: According to the Typikon, but not maintained today, the First Hour on Sundays is said in the narthex, and the brethren go there after the dismissal of Matins for the singing of the Gospel sticheron or other stichera (at the discretion of the ecclesiarch).

Appendix 2: According to modern practice, it is common, after the dismissal of the First Hour, for the troparion *Under thy merciful protection...* to be sung before the icon of the Mother of God. The ordering of any troparia sung at this point is the subject of diocesan regulations.

CHAPTER 2

The Third and Sixth Hours

1. The beginning of the Third and Sixth Hours is the same as that of all the divine services[1] as canonically laid down. When the priest has received a blessing from the bishop, if present, vested in stole and cuffs[2] and making three bows according to the order of making reverences, the priest begins the divine service,[3] saying aloud: *Blessed is our God....*

2. THE THIRD HOUR
The reader[4] of the Third Hour replies *Amen* and commences to read the "normal beginning," *Glory to Thee, our God..., Heavenly King...,* and Trisagion to the *Our Father.*

3. Priest: The normal exclamation, *For Thine is the kingdom...* and the reader says *Amen. Lord, have mercy* (twelve times), *Glory... Both now..., O come let us worship...* and reads the three psalms of the Third Hour, i.e., Psalms 16, 24, and 50. After Psalm 50, *Have mercy on me, O God...,* the reader, without any pause, says: *Glory..., Both now..., Alleluia...* (three times), *Lord, have mercy* (three times), and the troparia of the day. If it is a Sunday on which there is a commemoration of a saint, then after saying the triple *Lord, have mercy,* he reads the Sunday Troparion of the appointed tone. *Glory...,* and the troparion of the saint of that day.[5] If the service of a saint is not celebrated, then after the

40

triple *Lord, have mercy,* he reads the Sunday troparion of the appointed tone.

4. After reading the troparion, he reads: *Both now...,* and the Theotokion of the hour: *O Mother of God, thou art the true vine...,* the verse of the hour: *Blessed be the Lord God...,* and then straightaway the Trisagion to the *Our Father.* In the sanctuary, the priest pronounces the normal concluding exclamation to the *Our Father, For Thine is the kingdom....*

5. The reader answers *Amen,* and reads the Sunday kontakion of the appointed tone. He then immediately says the prayer: *Lord, have mercy* (forty times), and after this, the prayer: *Thou Who at all times and at every hour..., Lord, have mercy* (three times), *Glory..., Both now..., More honorable..., In the name of the Lord, Father give the blessing.* From the sanctuary the priest prays: *Through the prayers of our holy fathers....*[6]

6. The reader answers *Amen* and reads the Prayer of the Third Hour: *Master, God, Father Almighty....* This prayer completes the order of the Third Hour, and the Sixth Hour is begun straightaway.

7. THE SIXTH HOUR

Without any exclamation by the priest, because the blessing *Blessed is our God...* is treated as covering both the Third and Sixth Hours,[7] the reader starts to read: *O come, let us worship...* and the three psalms of the Sixth Hour, i.e., Psalms 53, 54, and 90. After Psalm 90, *He that dwells in the help of the Most High...,* the reader says: *Glory..., Both now..., Alleluia...* (three times), *Lord, have mercy* (three times). Immediately then, reading the troparia of the day. If it is a Sunday on which the service of a lesser saint is also celebrated, then he first reads the Sunday Troparion of the appointed tone, *Glory...* and the troparion of the saint given for that day.[8] If there is no service for a saint, then he reads *Glory*... and the Sunday Troparion of the appointed tone.

8. After reading the troparia, he reads, *Both now...*, the Theotokion of the hour: *Since we have no freedom to speak...*, the verse of the hour: *May Thy compassion...*, and immediately, Trisagion to the *Our Father.* The priest, from the sanctuary, pronounces the exclamation *For Thine is the kingdom...* and the reader reads the Sunday kontakion of the appointed tone.

9. After the kontakion, and as at all the Hours, he reads *Lord, have mercy* (forty times), the prayer: *Thou Who at all times and at every hour..., Lord, have mercy* (three times), *Glory..., Both now..., More honorable..., In the name of the Lord, Father give the blessing.*

10. From the sanctuary, the priest pronounces the exclamation: *Through the prayers...*, the reader: *Amen,* and he says the Prayer of the Sixth Hour: *O God and Lord of hosts....* This prayer should be read in an unhurried manner, quite slowly, because at this time the clergy before the altar in the sanctuary are making their immediate preparation to serve the Divine Liturgy. After the Prayer of the Sixth Hour, there is no dismissal of the Hours, because the Hours were celebrated in the church and not in the narthex, but the deacon now comes out of the north door onto the solea, and after his usual exclamation, the priest's exclamation begins the most important of all the services of the entire liturgical round, and of the whole Orthodox liturgical year, the service of the Divine Liturgy.

CHAPTER 3

The Divine Liturgy According to the Order of St John Chrysostom

1. At the appointed hour in the morning, the clergy come to the church. Entering into the sanctuary with reverence, the priest dons a stole and, having the deacon at his right side, stands before the holy table. Then, having made three bows from the waist and kissed the edge of the holy table, they go out of the sanctuary, the priest by the north door, the deacon by the south, and standing before the holy doors, they begin to read the Entry Prayers.[1]

2. When they have made three reverences with the words *O God, cleanse me, a sinner, and have mercy on me,* the deacon begins: *Master, give the blessing.*

The priest (quietly): *Blessed is our God...,* and the deacon begins to read the prayers of the normal beginning: *Amen. Glory be to Thee, O God..., O Heavenly King...,* and Trisagion to the *Our Father.* Then after the priestly acclamation *For Thine is the kingdom...,* he continues with *Amen* and the troparia[2] *Have mercy on us, O Lord, have mercy on us..., Glory be..., Lord have mercy on us..., Both now..., Open to us the doors of compassion....*

3. They then turn to the icon of the Savior, and the deacon says: *We venerate Thy most pure icon...,* while the priest, bowing to the ground before the icon, kisses it. At the end of the troparion, the deacon does likewise. Approaching the icon of the Mother of God, they perform the bows and kiss

43

it, while the deacon reads: *As a fountain of tenderness....* This done, as they stand before the holy doors, the deacon continues: *Let us pray to the Lord,* they bow their heads, and the priest reads the prayer: *Lord stretch forth Thy hand....* The deacon answers: *Amen.*

4. The clergy then bow to each other, after which they turn to face the people; bowing to them, they make one bow to the right and one to the left kliros, saying each time: *Forgive us and bless us, fathers and brothers,* and they go into the sanctuary.[3] Entering the sanctuary, they kiss the icons on the north or south doors (whichever they enter through), continuing to pray, *I will enter Thy house.*[4]

5. Coming into the sanctuary and standing before the table, they make three reverences, praying: *God cleanse me a sinner, and have mercy on me;* they kiss the holy Gospel, the holy cross, and the edge of the table and go to vest.

THE VESTING OF THE CLERGY

1. The deacon takes the stikharion and stole together in his right hand, makes three reverences toward the high place with the prayer: *God cleanse me a sinner...,* goes to the priest, and bowing his head continues: *Master, bless the robe and the stole.* The Priest blesses saying *Blessed be our God...* and places his hand upon the stikharion. The deacon kisses the hand that has blessed and goes to vest. When vesting, the deacon says the required prayers in the *Sluzhebnik.* At the stikharion, making the sign of the cross on himself, and kissing the cross on the stikharion, he says: *My soul rejoices in the Lord...* and robes in the stikharion. When he puts on the stole, he crosses himself, and kissing the cross upon the stole, says *Holy, Holy, Holy, Lord God of Sabaoth, heaven and earth are full of Thy glory*[5] and places the stole upon his left shoulder. When putting on the right cuff, he

crosses himself, and kissing the cross on the cuff, says *Thy right hand, O Lord...,* and puts the cuff on the right hand. When putting on the left cuff, he crosses himself, kisses the cross on the cuff, says *Thy hands have made me...,* and puts the cuff on the left hand.

2. Having vested, the deacon, saying the verses of Psalm 25, *I will wash my hands...,* washes his hands, and goes to the table of preparation to make ready the vessels and everything that is needed for celebrating the Liturgy of Preparation.[6] The deacon removes the covering from the table of preparation,[7] lights the candle or lamp upon the table,[8] takes the holy vessels, standing the holy paten to the left, and the holy chalice to the right on the table. The holy chalice must be placed on the table (and upon the holy table) reverently turned to show that side on which is found the image of the Savior (this side faces the priest; on the sides of the chalice are the images of the Mother of God and St John the Baptist and, on the back, the holy cross). The deacon then prepares the star, the spoon, lance, small veils, and aër. After this, he receives the prosphora from the server,[9] wine, and, a little apart, cups, small plates, and sponges.

3. The priest, after he has blessed the robe and stole of the deacon, also begins to vest. Taking the stikharion in his left hand, he makes three reverences toward the high place; blesses the stikharion, saying: *Blessed be our God...;* kisses the cross on it; and puts on the stikharion, saying in the same way as the deacon, *My soul rejoices in the Lord....* Taking the stole, he blesses it with the words *Blessed be our God...,* kisses the cross on the top of it, and puts it on with the prayer: *Blessed is God, Who pours out His grace....* Taking the girdle, and blessing it with the words, *Blessed be our God...,* he kisses the cross on it and girds himself with it, saying the prayer *Blessed be God Who girds*

me with strength.... He takes the right cuff, blesses it with the words *Blessed be our God...,* kisses the cross, and puts it on the right hand, saying the prayer: *Thy right hand....* He takes the left cuff, blesses it with the words *Blessed be our God...,* kisses the cross, and puts it on his left hand, saying the prayer: *Thy hands have made me....*

4. If the priest has been awarded the *nabedrennik,* he blesses it with the words *Blessed is our God...,* kisses the cross on it, arranges it on the right thigh, passing the cord under the girdle (if the priest has been awarded the *palitza* as well, the *nabedrennik* is worn on the left). If the priest has been awarded the *palitza,* he blesses it with the words *Blessed be our God...,* kisses the cross, and puts it on after the *nabedrennik,* on the right thigh. When vesting in the *nabedrennik* and the *palitza,* the priest says the same prayer over each: *Gird Thy sword....*

5. Taking the phelonion, the priest blesses it with the words, *Blessed be our God...,* kisses the cross on it, and puts it on, saying the prayer: *Thy priests, O Lord....* After this, saying the verses of Psalm 25, *I will wash my hands...,* he performs the customary hand washing.

THE LITURGY OF PREPARATION

6. Standing before the table of preparation, the priest and the deacon make three bows from the waist, saying the prayer:[10] *God cleanse me a sinner, and have mercy on me* and the troparion of Great Friday *Thou hast redeemed us from the curse of the law....* While reading this prayer, the priest kisses the Eucharistic vessels: at the words *Thou hast redeemed us...,* he kisses the discos; at the words *By Thy precious blood,* the chalice; at *Thou wast nailed to the cross,* the star; *and was pierced by a spear,* the lance; and at the words *Thou hast poured forth immortality...,* the spoon.

7. The deacon then says quietly: *Master, give the blessing*. The priest: *Blessed is our God....*[11] The deacon (quietly), *Amen*. The priest takes a prosphora in his left hand, to prepare the Lamb, and in his right hand, the lance.[12] With the lance, he traces the sign of the cross three times over the seal of the prosphora, saying each time: *In remembrance....* He then begins to cut the Lamb from the prosphora.

8. He cuts out the Holy Lamb from the bottom. It should not be forgotten that, in cutting the Lamb, he should not turn the prosphora, but at each cut place the lance so as to pierce each side in turn, the prosphora remaining stationary on the plate. The lance is held in three fingers, as one writes with a pen, and not with the full hand, as with an ordinary knife. This is not always possible, especially if the prosphora for the Lamb is large and thick. Then, for the removal of the Lamb, it is better to alter the position of the prosphora. One might lay it on the left side and cut the right from above, but one should not cut the prosphora from the left side.

9. If, because of a slip of the hand or from imperfections in the Lamb selected, it comes out unevenly, then, having taken it out, the priest should trim it on the plate and not on the discos.

10. It is good for the priest to take the Lamb out in this way so that the walls of the prosphora do not disintegrate.

11. Having blessed the prosphora for the Lamb, the priest takes out the Lamb as follows: The deacon says, *Let us pray to the Lord*, holding his stole with three fingers of the right hand, as when reading the litanies. The priest makes an incision in the right side of the prosphora (i.e., beside the letters **IC** and **NI**), saying: *He was led as a sheep to the slaughter*.

12. Deacon: *Let us pray to the Lord*. The priest makes an incision in the left side (beside the letters **XC** and **KA**), saying: *And as a lamb without blemish before its shearer is dumb,*

so He opens not His mouth. Deacon: *Let us pray to the Lord.* The priest makes an incision in the upper side (above the letters **IC** and **XC**), saying: *In His humiliation justice was denied Him.* The deacon: *Let us pray to the Lord.* The priest makes an incision in the lower side (below the letters **NI** and **KA**), saying: *Who shall declare His generation?* The deacon: *Take up, Master.* The priest makes an incision under the lower side of the prosphora and takes up the Lamb from the four cut sides, saying: *For His life is taken up from the earth.*

13. After this, the priest places the Lamb upon the paten with the seal downward. When turning the Lamb, he should take care not to turn it toward but away from himself. Also, the left side must be to the north, so that the turning of the seal may be an image of the passage of the sun. When piercing the Lamb, the lance needs to be held between the second and third fingers, so that the blade is toward the hand. The deacon says: *Sacrifice, Master.* The priest makes a deep incision with the lance (down to just beneath the seal of the Lamb), dividing the Lamb into four parts, but in such a way that the upper part, where the seal is to be found, is not pierced but only cut to the edge, and the priest says: *Sacrificed is the Lamb of God, Who takes away the sin of the world, for the life and salvation of the world.*

14. Having said these words, the priest places the Lamb with the seal upward, on the upper part of the paten. The Deacon says: *Pierce, Master.* The priest pierces the Lamb on the right side (the priest's left) and says: *One of the soldiers pierced His side with a spear, and at once, there came out blood and water. He Who saw it bore witness, and his witness is true.*

15. After this, the deacon takes the jug with wine, and having added water,[13] he offers it to the priest for blessing, saying: *Bless, Master, the holy union.* The priest blesses without saying anything,[14] and the deacon pours the mixture into the holy chalice.[15]

16. The priest sets about extracting the other particles from the remaining four prosphoras. From the second prosphora,[16] he extracts one particle in honor and memory of the Mother of God, saying as he does so: *In honor and memory*.... This particle is placed on the paten at the right side of the Lamb, that is to the priest's left, near to the middle of the Lamb, saying the words: *At Thy right hand*....

17. Then, taking the third prosphora, the priest, with the words: *Of the honored and glorious Prophet, Forerunner and Baptist, John,* takes a particle from it and places it on the left side of the Lamb, near its upper part. After this, the priest says: *Of the holy and glorious prophets...,* taking a second particle from the prosphora, placing it under the first, on the left side of the Lamb, a little distance from the Lamb, as with the first. The priest continues: *Of the holy, glorious and all-praised Apostles...* and takes a third particle from the prosphora, placing it beneath the second, on the left side of the Lamb, thus completing the first vertical row of particles.

18. The priest again says: *Of our fathers among the saints...* and, taking a fourth particle from the prosphora, places it level with the first particle, toward its left. The priest continues: *Of the holy Apostle...* and, taking the fifth particle, places it below the fourth to the left of the second. Continuing, the priest says: *Of our venerable and God-bearing Fathers...* and taking the sixth particle, places it below the fifth, to the left of the third, thus completing the second vertical row of particles.

19. Then the priest says: *Of the holy wonderworkers...* and, taking a seventh particle from the prosphora, places it above, to the fourth particle's left, so that it is level with the fourth and the first. Then the priest says: *Of the holy and righteous...* and, taking an eighth particle from the prosphora, places it below the seventh, to the left of the fifth.

At the taking out of this particle, it is normal to remember any other saints whose names are not given in the *Sluzhebnik.*[17] Then the priest says: *Of our father among the saints*... and, taking a ninth and final particle from the prosphora, places it below the eighth, to the left of the sixth, completing thus the third vertical row.

20. Taking a fourth prosphora, the priest extracts particles for the living from it. Taking the first particle, the priest says: *Remember, O Master*.... Taking the second particle, the priest says: *Remember Lord our God our protected country, our sovereign, lady Queen Elizabeth, and all Orthodox people.* These two particles are taken from the upper part of the prosphora at the corners below the seal. Then from this same prosphora[18] are taken out small particles for the living, circling from the right to the left of the upper part of the prosphora. At the taking out of these particles for the living, they are remembered by name with the words: *Remember, O Lord,* N. All the particles taken out in this way are placed on the lower part of the paten; moreover, the first two of them, for his Holiness the Patriarch and for the civil rulers, are placed above the other particles taken out for the health of the living.

21. Taking a fifth prosphora with the words: *In blessed memory...,* and remembering the bishop who ordained him (if he has died), the priest takes one larger particle from the middle of the prosphora, below the seal. And then out of the fifth prosphora, and any other prosphoras given by the faithful,[19] he takes out particles for the repose of the departed (in the same way as he did with the particles for the health of the living). Having finished the remembrance, the priest says: *Remember all our Orthodox fathers and mothers...* and places the particles for the repose of the departed upon the paten below the particles taken for the living.[20]

22. After all this, now that the priest has finished taking particles from the fifth prosphora, he again takes the fourth prosphora and takes out a particle for himself, saying this: *Remember also, O Lord, my unworthiness....* With the usual words *Remember, O Lord,* N, he follows the same process for any prayers for particular needs or for the special circumstances of the faithful. Such prayers may be found in the *Priestly Prayer Book* and the *Trebnik.*

[NB: Particles may be taken from the prosphoras for the living and for the departed until the time of the Great Entrance. The taking of particles for the living and for the departed after the Great Entrance is categorically forbidden (such particles should be kept until the next liturgy).]

23. Having remembered himself and placed his particle on the paten, the priest employs a sponge to gather all the particles of the Holy Bread away from the edge of the paten, so that none may fall off.

24. The server now gives a lighted censer to the deacon. The deacon takes it and, placing incense in it, presents it to the priest, saying: *Master, bless the incense. Let us pray to the Lord.* The priest, blessing the censer, says the prayer: *We offer Thee incense....*[21] The deacon holds the censer at the corner of the table of preparation to the right of the priest and says: *Let us pray to the Lord.*

25. The priest, taking the unfolded star, holds it over the censer, so censing it,[22] he then places it upon the paten, over the Lamb. At this, the priest says: *And the star came and stood over the place where the young child was.*

26. The deacon says: *Let us pray to the Lord. Cover Master.*[23] The priest takes the first small veil,[24] holds it in the censer's smoke, and then covers the paten with it, saying: *The Lord is King....* The deacon: *Let us pray to the Lord. Cover Master.* The priest takes the second small veil, holds it in the smoke of the censer, and covers the chalice with it, saying:

Thy virtue, O Christ.... The deacon: *Let us pray to the Lord. Cover Master.* The priest takes the aër, holds it over the censer in the smoke, and covers the veiled paten and the chalice with it, saying: *Cover us with the shelter of Thy wings....*

27. The deacon gives the censer to the priest, kissing his hand, and the priest censes the Holy Gifts three times, saying: *Blessed is our God...,* the deacon each time saying after him: *Always, now and for ever, and to the ages of ages. Amen.* When pronouncing these words, the priest and deacon bow three times toward the table of preparation. When the deacon has said for the third time *Always, now and for ever,* he takes the censer from the priest and calls him to pray, saying: *For the precious gifts here set forth, let us pray to the Lord.*

28. The priest, in a manner audible to the deacon, says the Prayer of the Prothesis: *O God, our God, Who didst send the heavenly bread...* and then says the normal dismissal. Priest: *Glory to Thee, O Christ our God....* Deacon: *Glory..., Both now..., Lord have mercy* (three times), *Give the blessing.* And the priest says the Lesser Dismissal: *May He Who is risen from the dead, Christ our true God...,* remembering the saint who has composed the liturgy for the day, for example, St John Chrysostom.

[*If more than one priest concelebrate, the junior normally carries out the preparation and, if there is no deacon, the initial censing of the church.*]

CENSING THE SANCTUARY AND THE CHURCH

29. After the Dismissal of the Liturgy of Preparation, the deacon, saying the troparion *In the tomb with the body...,* opens the curtain and makes the normal incensation of the holy table (on four sides).[25] Then, saying Psalm 50, he censes the sanctuary and the whole church in

the normal manner,[26] going out to the solea for the incensing by the north door and returning to the sanctuary by the south. He completes the censing as normal, i.e., he incenses the altar from the front, then the high place and the priest. He gives the censer to the server, makes a bow, standing at the east corner of the altar, to the high place, and then to the priest as he takes up his position beside the holy table.

30. If the Hours are still being read after the Dismissal of the Liturgy of Preparation, then the priest takes out particles from the prosphora offered by the faithful, and the deacon reads the memorial books and slips of paper sent into the sanctuary by the faithful. He continues to do so until the last exclamation of the Sixth Hour: *Through the prayers of our Holy Fathers....*

31. If he has not done so earlier, the deacon must, at this time, find the place in the Gospel book from which he is going to read during the liturgy.

32. When the reader of the Sixth Hour reaches the prayer *God and Lord of the powers...,* the priest and deacon stand before the holy table and bow down three times, saying the words: *God, cleanse me a sinner and have mercy on me.*

LITURGY OF THE CATECHUMENS

33. The priest holds up his hands in prayer, saying *O Heavenly King...,* the deacon meanwhile holding up the end of his stole with his right hand, as he does during the litanies.[27] After this prayer, both make a bow from the waist. The priest again lifts his hands and says twice: *Glory to God...,* bowing each time. Then a third time the priest with raised hands says: *O Lord, Thou shalt open my lips* and, having said that, kisses the holy Gospel, the deacon kissing the edge of the holy table.

34. The deacon, holding the stole with three fingers of his right hand and inclining the head, asks a blessing of the priest, saying: *It is time....* The priest blesses the deacon with these words: *Blessed be our God....* The deacon, having received the blessing, and again with inclined head, asks for the prayers of the priest for himself, saying: *Pray for me....* The priest responds: *May the Lord direct your steps.* Deacon: *Remember me, holy Master!*

35. Priest: *May the Lord remember....* The deacon replies *Amen* and, bowing[28] to the priest, leaves the sanctuary by the north door[29] and goes out onto the solea. Standing before the holy doors on the ambo (solea),[30] he bows three times, saying quietly: *O Lord, Thou shalt open my lips....* After this, lifting his stole, he says aloud: *Master, give the blessing.*

36. THE OPENING BLESSING OF THE LITURGY

The priest, holding the holy Gospel book, traces a cross with it upon the antimension, exclaiming: *Blessed is the kingdom....* The people: *Amen.* Having made the exclamation, the priest kisses the Gospel book and places it down upon the holy antimension.

37. THE GREAT LITANY

The deacon begins the Great Litany *In peace, let us pray to the Lord* (just as at the All-Night Vigil). Moreover, in the Great Litany (and equally in the Litany of Fervent Supplication), he may include any special intentions printed in the *Priestly Service-Books, The Book of Needs,* and in the different services authorized by ecclesiastical authority. In the Great Litany, these intercessions are made after the intercession *For those who travel...* and in such services, have associated with them proper troparia at the Entrance, Epistle and Gospel readings, and a communion verse. During the Great Litany, the priest in the sanctuary (before the holy throne[31]) quietly reads the Prayer of the First Antiphon: *O Lord our God...* and when the litany is finished, says aloud: *For to Thee belongs....*

[*When priests concelebrate without a deacon, the senior and presiding priest gives the opening blessing and says the first litany.*]

38. The First Antiphon of the Typika

The people: *Amen,* and they begin to sing the First Antiphon, drawn from Psalm 102. During the psalm (and indeed during the priestly exclamations), the deacon leaves the holy doors and stands before the icon of the Savior, holding his stole as usual, with three fingers of the right hand.

39. On Sundays, the antiphons of the Typika are drawn from Psalms 102 and 145[32] and the Beatitudes[33] (Matt 5:3–12). The First Antiphon, as the name implies, is sung antiphonally by the two choirs. The Typikon decrees that the entire antiphon be sung, each choir singing a verse (see the *Heirmologion*), coupling the first verse *Bless, the Lord, O my soul* with the response *Blessed art Thou, O Lord.* At the end of the antiphon, the first choir is to sing in a higher tone *Glory to the Father...,* the second choir, *Both now and for ever...,* and the first choir sings the first verse of the psalm: *Bless the Lord, O my soul, and all that is within me bless His holy name* and the response *Blessed art Thou, O Lord.*

40. The verses of the First Antiphon are then sung as follows:

First choir: *Bless the Lord, O my soul. Blessed art Thou, O Lord.*

Second: *Bless the Lord, O my soul and all that is within me bless His holy name.*

First: *Bless the Lord, O my soul: and forget not all His benefits.*

Second: *Who shows great mercy toward all thy sins, and heals all thy diseases.*

First: *Who redeems thy life from corruption; and crowns thee with mercy and loving kindness.*

Second: *Who satisfies thy desire amidst good things: thy youth shall be renewed as the eagle's.*

First: *The Lord is compassionate and merciful: long-suffering and of great mercy.*

Second: *Bless the Lord, O my soul: and all that is within me bless His holy name. Blessed are Thou, O Lord.*

41. When the singing of the antiphon is finished, the deacon stands before the holy doors and says the Short Litany *Again and again . . .* as normal. During the Short Litany, the priest in the sanctuary (before the throne) quietly reads the Prayer of the Second Antiphon: *Lord our God, save Thy people . . .* and at the completion of the litany says the exclamation: *For Thine is the dominion . . . .*

[*When there is no deacon at a concelebrated liturgy, the junior priest (or priests) says the two* Short Litanies.]

42. THE SECOND ANTIPHON OF THE TYPIKA

The choir sings *Amen* and begins to sing the Second Antiphon. During the priestly exclamation, the deacon again takes his place before the icon of the Savior where he stands for the duration of the whole second antiphon.

43. According to the Typikon, this antiphon is now sung in full, the second choir beginning:

Glory to the Father . . .[34] and then the first and second verses of the psalm: *Praise the Lord, O my soul . . . The Lord shall reign for ever, even Thy God, O Zion: from generation to generation.*

First choir: the response: *Both now and for ever . . . ,* immediately after which the people sing the hymn to Our Lord Jesus Christ: *Only-begotten Son and Word of God . . . .*

44. Regarding the hymn *Only-begotten Son,* the *Chinovnik* decrees another practice, both choirs singing the hymn together, but this is only at a hierarchical service (although for an especially effective Sunday service, this could also be done at an ordinary presbyteral service).

45. At the end of the singing of the hymn *Only-begotten Son,* the deacon, again standing before the holy doors, says the second Short Litany *Again and again....* According to established tradition, the deacon runs two petitions of the Short Litany together without a pause, the choir meantime singing *Lord have mercy* twice as one response. After the third petition, the choir sings *To Thee, O Lord, O Lord,* repeating for a second time the word *Lord*: this tradition being maintained in order to complete the musical phrase.

46. During the time of the second Short Litany, the priest quietly reads the Prayer of the Third Antiphon: *O Thou Who hast given us grace...* and at the end of the litany concludes with the exclamation: *For Thou, O God, art good....*

47. THE THIRD ANTIPHON OF THE TYPIKA

People: *Amen,* and they begin to sing the Third Antiphon, i.e., the Beatitudes. As the priest is saying the exclamation *For Thou, O God, art good,* the deacon bows and goes into the sanctuary by the south door; there he makes reverence before the holy throne, kissing the edge of the altar, and bowing to the high place and to the celebrating priest. He does this from the left side of the throne. At the beginning of the Third Antiphon,[35] the deacon opens the holy doors (if they were not opened at the exclamation *Blessed is the kingdom...*) and stands at the right side of the priest, awaiting the moment of the Entrance.

48. The Third Antiphon is begun by both choirs, with the troparia required by the Typikon.[36] As already noted, the Beatitudes are sung in the tone of the week, to a special

tune, similar to that of the troparia and canons. On Sundays, ten troparia are appointed to be sung on the Beatitudes; they are to be found in the Octoechos, at the end of the Sunday services of each tone.

> First Choir: *In Thy kingdom...for theirs is the kingdom of heaven.*
> Second Choir: *Blessed are those who mourn: for they shall be comforted.*
> First Choir: *Blessed are the meek...* and the first troparion from the Octoechos.
> Second Choir: *Blessed are those who hunger...* and the second troparion.
> First Choir: *Blessed are the merciful...* and the third troparion.
> Second Choir: *Blessed are the pure in heart...* and the fourth troparion.
> First Choir: *Blessed are the peacemakers...* and the fifth troparion.
> Second Choir: *Blessed are those who are persecuted...* and the sixth troparion.
> First Choir: *Blessed are ye...* and the seventh troparion.
> Second Choir: *Rejoice and be exceeding glad...* and the eighth troparion.
> First Choir:[37] *Glory...* and the ninth troparion.
> Second Choir: *Both now and for ever...* and the tenth troparion.

49. THE LITTLE ENTRANCE (ENTRANCE WITH THE GOSPEL BOOK)
Before the Third Antiphon ends, when the people begin to sing *Glory...,*[38] the priest and the deacon, standing before the holy table, make three bows, and the priest kisses the Gospel book, and the deacon, the edge of the holy table. The priest picks up the Gospel book from the holy table and gives it to the deacon. The deacon, with

the stole held in his right hand, takes the Gospel book, kissing the priest's hand. The priest now kisses the edge of the holy table and, the deacon leading and the priest behind, both go around the holy table and leave the sanctuary by the north door. They are preceded by the candle bearer (and where this is possible, not just one but two) with lighted candle in the candlestick. The deacon carries the holy Gospel in both hands. Coming onto the solea, all stand before the holy doors in the following order. The candle bearer, holding the candlestick in his hand or placing it down, stands near the icon of the Savior.[39] He faces north (if there are two candle bearers at the entrance, the second stands before the icon of the Mother of God, facing the first candle bearer[40]). The priest stands on the ambo (solea) before the holy doors, facing toward the holy table, the deacon stands before and to the right of the priest, half-facing the priest, and they both bow their heads. The deacon says quietly: *Let us pray to the Lord.* The priest quietly reads the Prayer of the Entrance: *O Master, Lord our God....*[41]

50. The deacon then stands before the holy doors, and again half-turning to the priest, places the Gospel book on his left shoulder and, holding it there with his left hand, with his right holding the stole, he points east, saying quietly to the priest: *Master, bless the holy Entrance.* The priest blesses, saying: *Blessed is the Entrance of Thy holy ones....* The deacon replies: *Amen,* takes the Gospel in both hands, and quickly moves it from his left shoulder and offers it to the priest to kiss. The priest puts both his hands on the Gospel book, kisses it, and the deacon in turn kisses the priest's hand and bows to him. Then holding high the Gospel book in both hands and turning around to the right toward the holy doors, he awaits the ending of the Third Antiphon.

51. At the end of the last troparion, lifting up the Gospel book, the deacon traces a sign of the cross and chants in a loud voice: *Wisdom! Stand aright!* Then he enters the sanctuary and places the holy Gospel on the holy table, in its normal place, that is, upon the holy antimension. Immediately after the deacon's exclamation, the people begin to sing the Entrance verse: *O come, let us worship...,*[42] and then the troparia and kontakia of the day. [*When there is no deacon at a concelebrated liturgy, the presiding priest carries the Gospel book and exclaims* Wisdom! Stand aright!]

52. While the Entrance verse is being sung, the priest enters the holy sanctuary. The candle bearer (or candle bearers) stands the candlestick before the holy doors and faces the holy table, awaiting the blessing of the priest.[43] The priest, having kissed the icon to the right of the holy doors, turns to face west and blesses the candle bearer.[44] Then he kisses the icon on the left side of the holy doors and goes to the holy table where, bowing, he kisses the Gospel and the edge of the altar. At the same time as the priest, the deacon also kisses the edge of the altar.

53. TROPARIA AT THE LITTLE ENTRANCE

The choirs now sing antiphonally the troparia and kontakia of the day. On Sunday, they begin by singing the Resurrection Troparion according to the appointed tone, then the troparion of the church if it is dedicated to the Mother of God or a saint,[45] and then the troparion of the saint of the day.[46] Afterward, they sing the kontakia. Beginning with the kontakion of Sunday in the appointed tone, the kontakion of the saint of the church, *Glory...,* kontakion of the saint of the day,[47] *Both now..., Protection of Christians....*[48]

54. While the troparia and kontakia are being sung, the priest quietly reads the Prayer of the Trisagion: *Holy God,*

Who art at rest.... At *Both now...,* the deacon draws near to the priest, bowing his head, and, holding the stole with three fingers of the right hand, says quietly to the priest: *Master, bless the time of the thrice-holy.* The priest blesses the deacon, the deacon kisses the hand that has blessed him, goes out of the holy doors onto the solea, and stands before them. When the people have finished singing the last kontakion, the priest, standing before the holy table, exclaims aloud: *For Thou, Our God, art holy... now and ever.*

[*This acclamation is always said by the presiding priest.*]

55. The deacon, standing on the solea before the holy doors and turning in the direction of the icon of the Savior, directs them with the stole, saying *O Lord, save the pious,* and then, turning to the right toward the people and pointing toward them with the stole held up in the right hand, slowly makes with his body a half-circle to his right (from the south, to the west, and then to the north), saying (slowly and solemnly) *And hear us;* he finishes the turn by facing toward the icon of the Mother of God. The people also chant: *O Lord, save the pious and hear us.* Turned toward the icon of the Mother of God and indicating her with his stole, after the singing of the choirs, the deacon proclaims: *And to the ages of ages.*

56. THE TRISAGION

The people answer *Amen* and begin to sing the hymn of the thrice-holy. The deacon goes through the holy doors into the sanctuary and stands alongside the priest, to his right, before the holy table. The choirs sing the Trisagion antiphonally:

First choir: *Amen. Holy God....*
Second: *Holy God....*
First: *Holy God....*
Second: *Glory..., Both now..., Holy and immortal....*
And the first choir finishes: *Holy God....*

57. During the singing of the Trisagion, the priest and the deacon bow three times before the holy table, saying (quietly), three times *Holy God....* The priest then kisses the Gospel book and the edge of the holy table;[49] the deacon kisses the edge of the holy table, and turning to the priest, says: *Command, Master.* They go to the high place, the priest saying the words: *Blessed is he that comes...;* going by the south side of the table, they come to stand then in the high place, the deacon to the north and the priest to the south. The deacon says: *Master, bless the throne on high,* and the priest blesses the high place with the words: *Blessed art Thou on the throne of glory....* The priest and deacon make a bow toward the high place, then to each other, and stand facing the worshippers. Here, the priest now blesses the reader of the Epistle. The reader, having received the blessing, goes out of the north door onto the solea and descends the steps of the ambo into the church. He then stands before the ambo, facing the holy doors. When going out of the sanctuary onto the ambo and proceeding to the place of reading, he takes the Epistle book in both hands, lifted before himself.[50] He then turns around to face east, lowers the Epistle book and opens it, and prepares to chant the prokeimenon.[51]

58. Reading of the Epistle

The deacon exclaims aloud from the high place: *Let us attend.* The priest, blessing the people from the high place, says: *Peace be with you all.* The reader, bowing, replies: *And with thy spirit.* The deacon: *Wisdom!* And the reader begins the prokeimenon: *Prokeimenon in the Nth tone,* and then the text of the prokeimenon. The first choir sings the prokeimenon in the named tone, the reader then pronounces the verse of the prokeimenon, and the second choir sings the same prokeimenon. Then the reader chants the first half of the prokeimenon, and the second choir continues with the second half of the prokeimenon. If two prokeimena are to be sung, then in place of the first half the reader announces: *The prokeimenon in the Nth tone* and the text of the second prokeimenon.[52] The first choir sings the second prokeimenon in that tone.

[*When priests concelebrate without a deacon, the president says:* Peace be with you all, *and the acclamations* Wisdom! *and* Let us attend! *at this and later points, are taken by the others.*]

59. Deacon: *Wisdom!* The reader announces the title of the Epistle reading.[53] The deacon: *Let us attend,* and the reader reads the Epistle.[54] During the reading of the Epistle, the server gives the censer to the deacon. Putting incense in it, the deacon holds up the censer before the priest: *Bless Master, the censer.* The priest blesses, saying the Prayer of the Censer, goes to the place prepared for him at the southeast side of the high place, and sits facing in the direction of the reading of the Epistle. The deacon begins to incense the holy table;[55] the prothesis; the sanctuary, as normal; then the holy doors. He then goes out onto the solea, censes toward the middle of the holy table, then the icons on the right side and the icons on the left side of the iconostasis. He goes through the holy doors, returning to the sanctuary, censes the priest at his seat (the latter stands and bows, and the deacon also responds to him with a bow). Then he censes those who stand within the sanctuary and goes again onto the solea, censes the reader of the Epistle, the left and right choirs, and then all standing in the church. Then, turning to the east, he censes the table, the icons of the Savior and the Mother of God, goes through the holy doors into the sanctuary, censes the seated priest (who does not rise), gives the censer to the server, and bows to the presiding priest (or the Rector).

60. If there are still many prosphora waiting, then the priest need not sit, but goes and extracts the particles from the prosphora, standing at the table of preparation.

61. At the last words of the Epistle reading, the priest stands, goes to the holy doors, and blesses the reader of the Epistle from the holy doors, saying to him: *Peace be with thee.* The reader: *And with thy spirit,* bowing as he is blessed.

62. The deacon: *Wisdom!* The reader begins to read the Alleluiarion: *Alleluia in the Nth tone,* or *Alleluia, Alleluia, Alleluia.* The choir, in the directed tone, begin to sing *Alleluia* three times. Reader: the proper verses (printed in the Epistle book after the prokeimenon). The choir again three times *Alleluia.* The reader: the next verse of the Alleluiarion. The choir: *Alleluia* three times. If there are two Alleluiaria, then they sing the first with verses and the second without.

63. THE READING OF THE GOSPEL

During the singing of the Alleluiarion, the deacon goes to the southwest corner of the holy table, the priest meanwhile, standing before the holy table, quietly reading the prayer: *O Master, Who lovest mankind....* After the prayer has been read, the deacon, holding the stole with three fingers of the right hand and with it indicating the holy Gospel, inclines his head and says quietly: *Bless, Master, him who proclaims....* The priest blesses him saying quietly: *May God, through the prayers...,* and kissing the holy Gospel, gives it to the deacon. The deacon: *Amen.* Bowing toward the holy Gospel, he takes it from the priest, kissing the priest's hand, and carries it through the holy doors onto the ambo. During the singing of the Alleluiarion, the server places an analoy on the ambo.

64. The priest, having given the Gospel book to the deacon, goes back to the high place and stands at its southeast

side. At the same time, the candle bearers go out of the north and south doors onto the solea; they light the candles and stand facing each other. On the solea, the deacon (going round the left side of the analoy and standing before it) places the Gospel book against his left shoulder and with his right hand lays the end of the stole on the analoy. He then places the Gospel book upon it and opens it, preparing to read. The candle bearers stand their candlesticks by the analoy[56] and again stand facing each other.

65. According to another tradition, the deacon, having taken the Gospel book from the priest, goes out on to the ambo, places his stole on the analoy, stands the Gospel book on the analoy, and holding it with both hands, exclaims aloud: *Bless, Master, him who proclaims....* Then, holding the Gospel book with both hands and laying his head upon it, waits until the end of the priest's exclamation. The priest, from the high place, blesses the deacon aloud: *May God, through the prayers...,* and the deacon says *Amen,* lays the Gospel book upon the analoy, and all then follows according to the normal order.

66. The priest, from the high place: *Wisdom! Stand aright! Let us listen to the holy Gospel. Peace be with you all,* blessing all the worshippers. People: *And with thy spirit.*

67. The deacon begins to read the title of the Gospel: *The reading is from the holy Gospel according to* N. People: *Glory to Thee, O Lord, glory to Thee.* Priest: *Let us attend.* The deacon reads the Gospel while the clergy and people stand with bowed heads.

68. At the end of the reading, the priest says quietly to the deacon: *Peace be with thee, who hast proclaimed the Gospel,* and goes to take it, proceeding from the high place by the north side of the table and standing in the holy doors.

69. The people: *Glory to Thee, O Lord, glory to Thee.* The deacon kisses the text of the Gospel (see the order of

the All-Night Vigil), closes the book, takes it, and the stole, from the analoy and carries it to the holy doors. The priest, at the holy doors, receives the Gospel book, and the deacon kisses the priest's hand and stands in his place for the reading of the Litany of Fervent Supplication. The priest places the holy Gospel on the holy table, standing it to the side of the antimension (to the south) in the uppermost part of the holy table.[57]

70. Meanwhile, when the priest blesses the deacon with the words *Peace be with thee...*, the candle bearers take their candlesticks from the analoy, and after the deacon has given the Gospel book to the priest, go back (each through his own door) into the sanctuary, with their lights.[58] The server meanwhile removes the analoy from the ambo.

[*When priests concelebrate without a deacon, a junior priest carries out the censing during the Epistle and the president reads the Gospel and the Litany of Fervent Supplication.*]

71. LITANY OF FERVENT SUPPLICATION

The deacon on the solea says the Litany of Fervent Supplication: *Let us all say....* When he reaches the petition *Again we pray for our sovereign lady...*, the priest reads the prayer: *O Lord our God, accept...*, and at the time of the petition for His Holiness the Patriarch, the priest unfolds the iliton and the antimension in three parts, but not opening the upper part of the antimension, which is done during the saying of the Litany for the Catechumens. At the end of the litany,[59] the priest pronounces the exclamation: *For Thou, O God, art merciful....*

72. LITANY FOR THE DEPARTED

At the time of the exclamation, the deacon goes into the sanctuary,[60] takes the censer from the server, places incense in it, and offers it to the priest for his blessing. The priest blesses the incense according to the normal manner,[61] and the deacon goes out onto the solea[62] to pronounce the Litany for the Departed.[63]

73. The deacon, standing before the holy doors censing: *Have mercy on us, O God* ... (and the rest of the litany). The priest in the sanctuary quietly reads the prayer: *O God of spirits and all flesh* .... During this prayer, the deacon goes back into the sanctuary,[64] censes the priest, and gives the censer to the server and remains at the usual side of the holy table.

74. When he has said the prayer, the priest exclaims: *For Thou are the resurrection....* The people reply, *Amen.* If the holy doors are still not closed, or if they were opened for the Litany for the Departed, in some churches the deacon now closes them. Then, proceeding around the north side of the holy table, the deacon goes out of the north door onto the solea to pronounce the Litany for the Catechumens.

75. LITANY FOR THE CATECHUMENS

The deacon, in front of the holy doors: *Catechumens, pray to the Lord*[65] and so on. At the petition *That He will reveal to them the gospel of righteousness,* the priest opens the upper edge of the iliton and the holy antimension. At the words *Catechumens, bow your heads to the Lord,* only any catechumens present, and not the faithful, bow their heads. The priest quietly reads the Prayer for the Catechumens: *O Lord our God, Who dwellest on high....* At the end of the litany, he exclaims aloud: *That with us they also....* At the exclamation, the priest takes the sponge (kept folded in the iliton with the antimension), makes a cross with it upon the antimension, kisses the sponge, and places it in the top right hand corner of the antimension, and then kisses the antimension.

THE LITURGY OF THE FAITHFUL

76. The deacon on the solea before the holy doors exclaims: *As many as are catechumens, depart ... in peace pray to the Lord.* With this exclamation, the deacon begins the First Litany of the Faithful. The people: *Lord have mercy.* During this litany, the priest in the sanctuary quietly reads the prayer: *We thank Thee, O Lord, God of the powers....* The deacon: *Wisdom!* The priest: *For to Thee belongs....* People: *Amen.*

77. The deacon says the Second Litany of the Faithful: *Again and again in peace....* During the litany, the priest quietly reads the prayer: *Again and many times....* Deacon: *Help us, save us....* People: *Lord have mercy.* Deacon: *Wisdom!* and, bowing, goes into the sanctuary by the north door,[66] bowing as normal to the holy table (coming to the edge of the table), the high place and the celebrating priest. The priest completes the prayer, exclaiming: *That being always guarded by Thy might....* At this exclamation, the deacon opens the holy doors (if they were closed), takes the censer from the server, and puts incense into it.

[*When priests concelebrate without a deacon, the junior priests take the litanies and exclamations after that of Fervent Supplication, and the president, the last before the Great Entrance.*]

78. CHERUBIC HYMN AND GREAT ENTRANCE

The choir sings *Amen* in a prolonged manner and then immediately begins to sing the Cherubic Hymn: *We Who in a mystery....*[67] The deacon, asking a blessing on the censer in the normal way, saying Psalm 50 quietly, censes the table, the sanctuary, and the solea, in the same order as at the censing during the Epistle reading. Having finished the censing, he gives the censer to the server and stands alongside the priest before the holy table.[68] While the deacon is censing, the priest quietly reads the Prayer of the Cherubic Hymn: *No one who is bound....*

[*When priests concelebrate without a deacon, the president carries out the censing at this point.*]

79. After the censing, the priest and the deacon, standing before the holy table, read the Cherubic Hymn quietly three times. The priest, lifting up his hands, prays: *We who in a mystery...* during which the deacon stands, holding up the stole with his right hand, and then, after the priest, completes the prayer: *That we may receive....* Then, making the sign of the cross, the priest and deacon bow before the holy table. They say this prayer and make the bows three times. Having read the Cherubic Hymn and bowed a third time, they kiss the holy table. The priest kisses the antimension and the edge of the holy table, the deacon just the edge of the holy table. They then bow to each other and then to the worshippers, and after this they go to the table of preparation. According to the *Sluzhebnik,* the deacon goes in front of the priest.[69]

80. The priest takes the censer and incenses the Holy Gifts, saying quietly three times: *God, cleanse me a sinner....* Having censed the gifts, he gives the censer to the deacon. The deacon says: *Lift up, Master.* The priest takes the aër covering the chalice and the paten and places it on the left shoulder of the deacon with the words: *Lift up your hands in the holy place and bless the Lord.* The deacon kneels on one knee (the right); taking the censer by placing the ring of the censer on one of the fingers of his right hand and holding it over the right shoulder, he then turns to the priest, saying: *May the Lord God remember thy priesthood....* The priest takes the paten, kisses it over the veil and star, and standing with the paten, he says: *May the Lord God remember thy diaconate....* He places the paten on the head of the

deacon, and the deacon, taking the paten with both hands, rises from his knees.[70]

81. With the words: *Remember me, O Lord, when Thou comest in Thy kingdom,* the priest takes the holy chalice, kissing it over the veil, and holding it with the fingers of the right hand, comes behind the deacon onto the solea by the north door.

[*When priests concelebrate without a deacon the president carries the chalice, and another the paten.*]

82. There now begins the Great Entrance proper, that is, the procession of the Holy Gifts from the table of preparation to the holy table. Ahead of the celebrating clergy go two candle bearers with lighted candles, then the deacon with the holy paten and the censer, followed by the priest with the holy chalice. When they have come out of the north door onto the solea, the candle bearers go down from the ambo and stand facing the holy doors, not putting down their candlesticks. The deacon and the priest stand in the middle of the solea, before the holy doors, facing the people. The people, candle bearers, singers, and readers bow their heads (they do not bow to the ground as in the Liturgy of the Presanctified Gifts).[71]

83. Standing facing the worshippers, the deacon exclaims: *Our Lord and Father*... and, having remembered the Patriarch of Moscow and all Rus' and the bishop of the diocese,[72] he goes into the sanctuary through the holy doors, turning to his left (to the south and then to the east), and remains at the southwest side of the table, kneeling on one knee, holding the paten on his head. The priest, immediately after the deacon, says: *You and all Orthodox Christians... and to the ages of ages,*[73] and, turning to the left, goes into the sanctuary through the holy doors.[74]

84. The candle bearers take and lift their candlesticks, standing with them before the holy doors, and remain facing

the holy table. The priest, going into the sanctuary, kisses the chalice through the veil and places it upon the opened antimension. The deacon, addressing the priest, says: *May the Lord God remember thy priesthood in His kingdom.* To this the priest replies: *May the Lord God remember thy diaconate in His kingdom, always....* He then takes the paten from the deacon's head, kisses it through the veil and star which are over the paten, and places them on the left side of the chalice on the open antimension, saying these troparia: *Noble Joseph..., In the tomb with the body...,* and *Truly Thy tomb, O Christ....* The priest takes the veils off the paten and chalice and places them on the corners of the holy table:[75] that from the paten to the northwest and that from the chalice to the southwest.

85. During this, the deacon goes to the holy doors and censes the candle bearers, after which they, bowing, go in by their respective doors, taking with them the candlesticks. The deacon then closes the holy doors and draws the curtain across,[76] and turning round, stands in his place to the right of the priest.

[*When priests concelebrate without a deacon, a junior priest closes the curtain and pronounces the next litany.*]

86. The priest, taking the aër from the deacon's shoulder, holds it over the censer, which is held by the deacon. He covers the chalice and paten with the aër, quietly saying: *Noble Joseph....* The deacon gives the censer to the priest, who censes the gifts and says: *Be favorable, O Lord....* Giving the censer to the deacon, the priest addresses him with the words: *Remember me, brother and fellow minister.* The deacon, taking the censer, answers the priest: *May the Lord God remember thy priesthood in His kingdom,* and gives the censer to the server.

87. After this, the deacon, taking and lifting the end of his stole with three fingers of the right hand and bowing

the head, addresses the priest: *Pray for me, holy Master.* The priest replies: *The Holy Spirit shall come upon thee...* The deacon, addressing the priest, says: *The Spirit Himself will minister...* and *Remember me, holy Master.* The priest: *May the Lord God remember thee...* and the deacon completes the dialogue with: *Amen.*

88. The people, after the priest's exclamation: *You and all Orthodox Christians...*, sing the second part of the Cherubic Hymn: *Amen. That we may receive...*, finishing the hymn by singing three times, *Alleluia.*[77]

89. LITANY OF SUPPLICATION

In the sanctuary, the priest blesses the deacon, who kisses his hand and goes around the holy table, saluting the edge of the table in the usual way, and goes out of the north door for the first Litany of Supplication: *Let us complete our prayer to the Lord.* The people answer the deacon's petition: *Lord have mercy.* Deacon: *For the precious gifts..., For this holy house..., For our deliverance..., Help us, save us...*, and then through the rest of the litany as normal (see All-Night Vigil), saying as the next petition: *That the whole day....*

90. During the litany, the priest quietly reads the Prayer of Offering: *O Lord, God Almighty, Who alone art holy....* At the end of the litany, the priest says aloud: *Through the compassion....* People: *Amen.*

91. The priest blesses the faithful: *Peace be with you all.* The people: *And with thy spirit.* The deacon, on the solea: *Let us love one another....* People: *Father, Son and Holy Spirit...*, while the priest in the sanctuary makes three bows, saying each time: *I will love Thee, O Lord my strength...*, he then kisses the paten and the chalice (through the aër) and the edge of the holy table, and, making a sign of the cross, then opens the curtain.

92. THE CREED

The deacon makes a sign of the cross, kisses the cross at the end of his stole, and exclaims: *The doors, the doors! In wisdom let us attend.* The singing of the Creed is begun:[78] *I believe in one God....* During the Creed, the priest takes the aër from off the vessels and with both hands fans it over the paten and chalice, saying the Creed in an undertone. At the end of the Creed, he kisses the aër, folds it, and places it under the veils on the left side of the holy table.

93. THE EUCHARISTIC CANON

At the end of the Creed, the deacon exclaims, standing before the holy doors: *Let us stand aright....* People: *Mercy and peace, a sacrifice of praise.* After this exclamation, the deacon bows and goes into the sanctuary by the south door, bows to the high place and to the celebrating priest, and stands with him at the southwest of the holy table.

94. The priest turns to the people and blesses them, saying: *The grace of our Lord, Jesus Christ....* People: *And with thy spirit.* The priest, lifting his hands:[79] *Let us lift up our hearts.* People: *We lift them up unto the Lord.* Priest: *Let us give thanks unto the Lord.* Having made this exclamation, the priest bows down to the ground before the holy table. People: *It is meet and right....*

95. After the priest's exclamation, the deacon goes around the table, from its south to the north side, kisses the edge of the holy table, bows to the priest, and stands alongside him. The priest quietly reads the prayer: *It is meet and right to hymn Thee....* Then at the end, aloud: *Singing, crying, shouting....*

96. At these words, the deacon takes the stole with three fingers of the right hand, and then the star, and then when the priest utters the word "crying," touches the star to the east part of the paten, then at "shouting" to the west, at "the

triumphal hymn" to the north, and at "and saying" to the south. Then he kisses the star, putting it, unfolded,[80] on the east side of the table, over the veils. He makes a bow to the high place and to the priest, goes around the table, and stands to the right of the priest. After the exclamation, the people sing: *Holy, Holy, Holy*.... The priest continues quietly reading the prayer: *With these blessed powers, O Master... He gave it to His holy disciples and Apostles, saying:* The priest then says aloud: *Take eat, this is my Body...,* and stretching out the right hand with the palm upward, holding the fingers together, indicates the Holy Bread, lying on the paten. The deacon, likewise holding the stole with three fingers of the right hand, indicates the paten. People: *Amen.*

97. The priest, quietly: *In the same way also, after supper, He took the cup saying,* and aloud: *Drink from this, all of you...,* and indicates the chalice with his right hand as he did the paten. The deacon again indicates the chalice with the stole in his right hand. The people, in a prolonged fashion, *Amen.* During the latter, the priest reads: *Remembering therefore...,* and then aloud: *Offering Thee Thine own of Thine own...,* during which the deacon, folding his hands in the form of a cross (right over left), holds in the right hand the chalice and in the left the paten and elevates the holy things.[81] The deacon puts them down again on the holy antimension and stands alongside the priest. The people sing: *We hymn Thee, we bless Thee....*

98. The priest now prays: *Again we offer Thee this reasonable worship....* Bowing three times before the holy table, the priest and deacon pray: *O God, cleanse me, a sinner, and have mercy on me.* Then the priest, lifting his hands (while the deacon holds up the stole with his right hand): *O Lord, Who at the third hour....* The deacon prays after the priest: *Create in me a clean heart...,* and after that the priest and deacon, making the sign of the cross, bow down before

the holy table. The priest prays again with upraised hands (the deacon holding up his stole): *O Lord, Who at the third hour*.... Deacon: *Cast me not away from thy presence...*, and again making the sign of the cross, they once more bow to the ground before the holy table. Then the priest prays a third time (both he and the deacon lifting the hands as before): *O Lord, Who at the third hour*.... The deacon, bowing his head and pointing to the discos with his stole: *Master, bless the Holy Bread*. The priest pronounces the words: *And make this bread...*, blessing the Holy Bread with the right hand. (It is not fitting that the hand blessing should go further than the edge of the paten. Besides which, the Holy Bread needs to be blessed in such a way, because the blessing is made upon it alone and not over the other particles round about it.)[82]

99. The deacon replies *Amen*, and pointing to the chalice with his stole, says: *Master, bless the holy cup*. The priest blesses the holy chalice with the words: *And that which is in this cup*.... Again the hand blessing must not do so outside the lip of the chalice. The deacon replies: *Amen*, and with his stole, points to the Holy Gifts, saying: *Master, bless them both*.

100. The priest, with a larger gesture of blessing, blesses the bread and the wine in a single movement, saying: *Changing them by thy Holy Spirit*. The deacon: *Amen, Amen, Amen*. And they bow down to the ground before the Holy Gifts.

101. Standing upright, the deacon takes the stole in three fingers of the right hand and, inclining the head, addresses the priest: *Remember me, Holy Master*. The priest: *May the Lord God remember thee...*, and the deacon answers: *Amen* and goes to his former place.[83] The priest quietly reads the prayer: *So that for those who partake... and every righteous spirit made perfect in faith.*

102. The deacon takes the censer from the server and, toward the end of the prayer, gives it to the priest. The priest, taking the censer from the deacon, censes three times before the holy table[84] and says aloud: *Especially for our most holy....* Having pronounced the exclamation, he gives the censer back to the deacon, and the deacon censes the holy table from the other three sides[85] and gives the censer to the server.

103. HYMN TO THE MOTHER OF GOD

People: *It is truly meet...*[86] or other hymn to the Mother of God appointed by the Typikon. During the singing of the hymn, the priest prays quietly: *For the holy Prophet... in all godliness and holiness.*[87] And, at the end of this prayer of commemoration, he exclaims: *Among the first... the word of thy truth.* People: *And each and all.* The priest quietly continues praying:[88] *Remember, O Lord... and upon us all send down Thy mercies.*[89] Then audibly: *And grant that with one mouth....* The people reply: *Amen.*

104. The priest, turning toward the west, blesses the people, saying: *And the mercies....* People: *And with thy spirit.*

105. LITANY BEFORE THE LORD'S PRAYER

The deacon, standing at the southeast side of the table, now bows to the high place and to the priest and, having received his blessing, goes around the holy table by the north door onto the solea for the Litany before the Lord's Prayer. The deacon, standing on the solea before the holy doors: *Having remembered all the saints....* During the Litany before the Lord's Prayer, the priest in the sanctuary quietly prays: *To Thee, O Master Who lovest mankind....* At the end of the litany, after the petition *For a Christian end...,* the deacon says the petition: *Having asked for the unity of the faith....* People: *To Thee, O Lord.*

[*When there is no deacon, this litany is said by a priest other than the president, but the latter says:* And count us worthy....]

106. THE LORD'S PRAYER

The priest before the holy table, lifting his hands, exclaims: *And count us worthy, O Master....* The people sing: *Our Father....* While it is being sung, the deacon, standing before the icon of the Savior, wraps the stole around him in the form of a cross.[90]

107. The priest, at the end of the singing of the Lord's Prayer, exclaims aloud as normal: *For Thine is the kingdom....* People: *Amen.* Then, turning around and facing the people, the priest blesses them, saying: *Peace be with you all.* The people reply: *And with thy spirit.* The deacon: *Bow your heads to the Lord.* The people sing in an extended manner: *To Thee, O Lord,* during which the priest quietly reads the prayer: *We thank Thee, O King invisible ... our souls and bodies.* And then aloud: *Through the grace and compassion....* People, in an extended manner: *Amen* while the priest reads the following prayer quietly: *Give heed, O Lord Jesus Christ our God....* After this, he bows three times before the holy table, praying: *O God, cleanse me, a sinner, and have mercy on me.* (Once at each bow.)

108. The deacon, on the solea, also makes three bows simultaneously with the priest, praying in the same words, and then says: *Let us attend.* At this exclamation, the priest closes the curtain and then turns back to the holy table. The deacon enters the sanctuary by the south door. Going into the sanctuary, he bows to the high place and to the priest and stands to the southeast of the table. The priest takes the Holy Lamb with both hands,[91] lifts it above the paten, and says aloud: *The holy things for the holy.*[92]

109. THE COMMUNION

The people: *One is holy, one is Lord...*, and they sing the communion verse of the day. On Sundays: *Praise the Lord from heaven, praise him in the highest* is appointed.[93] If it is the feast of a saint that day, then the communion chant of that day is used as well (i.e., if it is a saint's day with an appointed Epistle and Gospel). So, after the communion verse of Sunday, that of the saint is sung.[94] After the singing of all the communion chants appointed for that day, the people sing three times, *Alleluia*.[95] There is a tradition of singing the communion chant antiphonally.[96] As the communion chants begin to be sung, a candle bearer stands a lighted candle before the holy doors.

110. COMMUNION OF THE CLERGY

After the exclamation *The holy things for the holy*, the deacon, standing before the holy table, turns to the priest and says: *Master, divide the Holy Bread.* The priest, with attention and reverence, breaks the Holy Bread,[97] quietly saying: *Broken and distributed....* He then places the portions of the Holy Bread on the paten in a crosswise fashion: the portion with the seal **IC** on the east side of the paten; the portion sealed **XC** on the west (lower) side; the portion marked **NI** on the north (left) side; and that sealed **KA** on the south (right) side.[98]

111. The deacon points with the stole to the holy chalice and says: *Master, fill the holy cup.* The priest takes[99] the portion sealed **IC** from the paten, makes a sign of the cross with it over the chalice, and places it in the holy chalice,[100] saying: *The fullness of the Holy Spirit.* The deacon says *Amen.* The server hands the deacon the cup with hot water.[101] The deacon, taking the cup from the server and holding it with both hands, conveys it to the priest, making a bow from the waist[102] without a sign of the cross, and

proffers it to the priest, saying: *Master, bless the hot water.* The priest blesses it with the words: *Blessed is the fervor of Thy holy things...Amen.* After the priest has blessed the hot water, the deacon pours it cross-wise into the holy chalice, saying: *The fervor of faith, full of the Holy Spirit. Amen.* Having done this, the deacon hands the cup back to the server and makes a bow from the waist with a sign of the cross.

112. The deacon now goes to the high place and stands facing the priest. They both make three bows from the waist, with the words: *God, cleanse me a sinner....* After these three bows, they say the prayer: *Loose, remit, and pardon, O God....* Then they bow to the ground before the holy table,[103] bow to each other, to all who are worshipping in the sanctuary, and afterward—to the west—to all who are worshipping in the church, each time saying: *Forgive me, fathers and brothers.*[104] After this, the priest again bows to the ground before the Holy Gifts, saying: *Behold I draw near to my immortal King and God.*

113. The priest then calls the deacon with the words: *Deacon, draw near.* The deacon goes around the holy table to the north side, and with the words: *Behold, I draw near...,* he bows to the ground and kisses the edge of the holy table, goes to the priest, and says: *Give me, Master...,* holding his hands before him in the following manner: palms upward, the right hand over the left.

114. The priest takes a particle (broken earlier from the portion **IC**) and gives it to him with the words: *The Deacon N....* The deacon takes the particle in the palm of the right hand and kisses the hand that gave it and the right shoulder of the priest. The priest greets the deacon with the words: *Christ is in our midst.* The deacon replies to the greeting: *He is and shall be.*[105] And goes back by the north to the east of the holy table, where, inclining his head and holding his hands

upon the holy table, he awaits the reading of the Prayers before Holy Communion.[106]

115. The priest kisses the edge of the holy table, takes a particle of the Holy Body with his left hand, placing it in his right palm with the words: *The precious and most Holy Body...,* and, bowing his head, makes ready to read the Prayers before Holy Communion.

116. Then the priest and deacon with bowed heads pray simultaneously: *I believe Lord, and I confess...* and after that, in the fear of God, communicate in the Holy Body of Christ. Having received, the priest takes the sponge from the antimension and, with it, wipes the palm of his right hand over the discos. At the same time, the deacon, standing at the table, gathers together any crumbs of the Holy Lamb that may be adhering to his palm and consumes them.

117. The priest then takes the communion cloth (as a precaution against spilling any drop of the Holy Blood) and tucks one end of it into the upper edge of the phelonion. He keeps the other end of the cloth in his hand, and then with both hands takes the chalice and sips three times of the Holy Blood from it, first pronouncing: *The precious and Holy Blood....* Normally, at the three-fold communicating of the Holy Blood, the celebrating priest says: *In the name of the Father, and of the Son, and of the Holy Spirit. Amen.*[107]

118. After communicating, the priest wipes his lips and the edge of the chalice with the cloth, and then kisses the edge of the chalice and says: *This has touched my lips....* Furthermore, kissing the chalice, the priest then says three times: *Glory be to Thee, O God.*

119. The priest calls the deacon with the words: *Deacon, draw near.* The deacon comes to the priest and bows, saying: *Behold I draw near...,* and then says to the priest: *Give me, Master....* With his left hand, he takes one end of the cloth and holds it under his chin; holding the other end of

the cloth with his right hand, he makes ready to receive the chalice. The priest conveys the holy chalice to the deacon (holding it with both hands); the deacon steadies the chalice with his right hand, and the priest communicates the deacon in the Holy Blood with the words: *The servant of god, Deacon N*.... The deacon drinks of the Holy Blood three times and then, with the cloth in his hand, wipes his lips and the edge of the holy chalice, after which he kisses it. The priest, meanwhile, says: *This has touched thy lips*....

120. After this, the priest stands the holy chalice in its place on the antimension and reads the Prayer of Thanksgiving: *We thank Thee, O Master, Who lovest mankind*... and starts to divide the portions of the Lamb sealed with **NI** and **KA**. Reading the hymns: *We have seen the resurrection of Christ*..., he divides these portions into little particles, as many as necessary for all the communicants. Then the priest places all these particles into the chalice, covers the chalice with a small veil, and puts the spoon on top; the paten is covered with the star and the other small veil.[108]

121. After filling the chalice with the particles and having said the prayers appointed, the priest goes to the table of preparation, and takes a drink of blessed hot water and eats some antidoron (prosphora).

122. COMMUNION OF THE LAITY

When it is time for the communion of the laity, the server takes the candle from in front of the holy doors.[109] The priest, approaching the holy table, picks up the chalice and turns to face the west. The deacon, meanwhile, draws the curtain aside and opens the holy doors, takes the communion cloth, and turns to face the priest. The priest kisses and gives the holy chalice to the deacon. Holding the chalice, the deacon turns to face the people, and they go through the holy doors to their place on the solea. The deacon, holding aloft the holy chalice, exclaims: *With fear of God, with faith and love, draw near.* The people sing *Blessed is he that comes...* and the deacon gives the chalice to the priest.[110]

[*When priests concelebrate without a deacon, the president takes the chalice and says* With fear of God ...; *he also gives communion and says everything else up to and including* Blessed is our God....]

123. The priest reads the Prayers before Communion (not hastily, aloud, but not chanted): *I believe, O Lord, and I confess....* At the end of the prayers, the communicants make the sign of the cross, bow to the ground, and cross their hands on the breast (right hand over left), and they go to the holy chalice, giving their names.

124. Proper order must be kept at the holy chalice during communion. The communicants must approach only from the south side of the church. The north side must always be left free for the worshippers to reach the small table with the *zapivka* and antidoron.[111] Moreover, it is better that the space before the solea also be kept free, so that only the person communicating is there.

125. The communicants go to the holy chalice in the following order: First the infants come to communion,[112] then the children (up to age fifteen), then come the men, and after that the women. It is important that all be aware of the care to be taken at the holy chalice, be they clergy, assistants, or all the faithful in general. There should be no pushing, shoving, or ill-intentioned attempts to touch the Holy Gifts.

126. The choir, during the time of the communion of the people, sing: *Receive the Body of Christ....*

127. When the priest communicates an infant, he says: *The infant, N, receives the most pure Blood of our Lord, God, and Savior Jesus Christ for the sanctification of soul and body and to eternal life,* and he gives a few drops of the Holy Blood from the tip of the spoon.

128. When adults (or teenagers) are communicating, the priest says: *The servant of God,*[113] N, *receives the most precious and Holy Body and Blood of our Lord Jesus Christ, for the remission of sins and life eternal.* Without rushing, he gives the Holy Gifts on the spoon, into the mouth of the one communicating, and as soon as the communicant has tasted, he withdraws the spoon.

129. The deacon[114] wipes the mouth of the communicants with the cloth, and the communicant, having kissed the edge of the holy chalice without grasping it, goes to the small table for the warm wine and water and also partakes of antidoron. (See Chapter 32 of the Typikon.)

130. After the communion of the laity, the priest and deacon go back into the sanctuary,[115] and the priest[116] places the chalice on the holy antimension. People: *Alleluia, Alleluia, Alleluia.*

131. Having placed the Holy Gifts upon the table, the priest turns to the people[117] and blesses them, saying: *O God, save Thy people, and bless Thine inheritance.* People: *We have see the true light....*

132. Meanwhile, the deacon, taking his place before the table instead of the priest, reads: *We have seen the resurrection of Christ..., Shine, shine...,* and *O Christ, great and most holy Pass-over....* He takes the holy paten and, wiping it with the sponge from the antimension, he brushes the commemorative particles that were lying upon the paten into the chalice, saying: *Wash away, O Lord, by Thy precious Blood the sins of Thy servants here remembered, through the prayers of the Mother of God and of all Thy saints.*[118] The deacon then covers the chalice with a small veil and places the star, lance, and spoon on the paten and covers them with the second small veil.

133. Having blessed the people, the priest reads the Prayer of Thanksgiving quietly before the holy table:

We thank Thee, O Master, Who lovest mankind.... The server gives the deacon the censer, the deacon presents it to the priest, and the priest, putting incense into it and giving the usual blessing, censes the Holy Gifts three times, saying quietly: *Be Thou exalted, O God, above the heavens: and Thy glory over all the earth.* Having censed the Holy Gifts, he gives the censer to the deacon. The deacon takes the censer in his left hand and, according to one tradition, kneels on one knee before the holy table. The priest takes the paten from the holy table and places it on the deacon's head. Taking the paten with the right hand, the deacon stands and goes around the table by the west and north sides to the preparation table, turning toward the people as he does so. Reaching the preparation table, he stands the paten upon it and, taking the censer in his right hand, censes the Holy Gifts as the priest comes and lays them upon the preparation table.

134. The priest, bowing before the Holy Gifts, takes the holy chalice, kisses it, and turns to face the people, quietly saying: *Blessed is our God.* Standing facing west in the holy doors, he exclaims aloud: *Always, now and for ever, and to the ages of ages.*[119] The people: *Amen. Let our mouth be filled....*

135. Having pronounced the exclamation, and saying: *Be Thou exalted, O God, above the heavens: and Thy glory over all the earth,* the priest goes to the table of preparation and places the holy chalice upon it. The deacon gives the censer to the priest, and the priest censes the Holy Gifts on the preparation table, making a bow before them. He then gives the censer to the deacon, who gives it to the server.

136. The priest returns to the holy table and takes the sponge from the antimension. He makes a sign of the cross with it upon the antimension, kisses the antimension and the sponge, and then places the sponge in the middle of the antimension, which he closes (together with the iliton): first

the upper part, and then the lower, then the left, and finally the right.

137. The deacon unwraps his stole, placing it as before upon his left shoulder, and goes out of the north door on to the solea to pronounce the Litany of Thanksgiving.

138. THE LITANY OF THANKSGIVING AFTER COMMUNION

Standing before the open holy doors, the deacon begins the litany: *Stand aright. Having received....*[120]

The priest takes the Gospel book and, holding it upright, makes the sign of the cross over the antimension with it, exclaiming: *For thou art our sanctification...,* and places the Gospel book down upon the antimension. People: *Amen.* During this exclamation, the deacon goes to his place before the icon of the Savior.

[*When priests concelebrate without a deacon, a junior says this litany but the president says the exclamation* For thou art our sanctification....]

139. PRAYER BEHIND THE AMBO

The priest exclaims: *Let us go forth in peace* and goes out of the holy doors, across the solea to below the ambo, to read the Prayer behind the Ambo. The people: *In the Name of the Lord.*

The deacon, before the icon of the Savior, looking toward the priest with the stole in his right hand, says: *Let us pray to the Lord* and bows his head; with the stole lifted, he stands thus before the icon until the end of the Prayer behind the Ambo. People: *Lord have mercy.*

[*When priests concelebrate, the junior priest says:* Let us go forth... *and the Prayer behind the Ambo.*]

140. The priest says the prayer: *O Lord, Who blessest those who bless Thee... and to the ages of ages.* People: *Amen* and *Blessed be the Name of the Lord...* (thrice),[121] and then

follows the Psalm 33 (unabridged): *I will bless the Lord at all times....*[122]

141. After the prayer, the priest returns to the sanctuary by the holy doors, and after him, the deacon, crossing the solea, returns through the north door to the table of preparation.

142. Consumption of the Holy Gifts

The priest, having entered the sanctuary, reads the prayer at the consumption of the Holy Gifts before the holy table: *Christ our God, Who art thyself the fulfillment...*, and the deacon, bowing his head before the holy table, listens to it and answers the priest: *Amen.* The priest then blesses the deacon, the sign of the cross being made on the deacon's head, which is laid on the edge of the holy table, after which the deacon goes to the preparation table. There he takes the cloth, tucks one end of it into the upper edge of his stikharion, and with the other holds the chalice with his left hand, while with the right hand he holds the spoon with which he consumes all the contents of the chalice. He then rinses the holy chalice a few times with hot water, until not even the smallest particle of the Holy Bread remains on the sides. Then, drinking this water, he wipes dry the chalice with the sponge[123] and, with the cloth, the spoon. Having completed this, he puts all the Eucharistic vessels away in the sacristy.

143. Dismissal of the Liturgy

Having blessed the deacon, the priest, at the end of Psalm 33, stands at the holy doors facing the people, blessing them with the words: *The blessing of the Lord be upon you....* People: *Amen.* And then he gives the Dismissal of the Divine Liturgy.

144. The priest: *Glory to Thee, O Christ our God and our hope, glory to Thee.* People: *Glory..., Both now..., Lord*

have mercy (thrice), *Give the blessing.* And the priest says the proper dismissal: *May [He Who has risen from the dead,] Christ our true God, through the prayers of His most pure Mother, of the holy, glorious and all-praised Apostles, of our father among the saints John Chrysostom, Archbishop of Constantinople, and saint* (the saints of the church[124] and of those whose day it is), *of the holy and righteous forebears of God, Joachim and Anna, and of all the saints, have mercy on us and save us, for He is good and loves mankind.*[125] The people, the Many Years: *To our great Lord and Father* .... This concludes the Divine Liturgy. The priest offers the precious cross to the people to kiss, and then returns to the sanctuary, closes the holy doors, and draws the curtain.

145. The deacon, having consumed the Holy Gifts, reads the Prayers of Thanksgiving after Holy Communion and the troparia[126] directed by the Typikon, and then removes and puts away his vestments in the sacristy of the church.[127] The priest, having returned to the sanctuary, like the deacon, reads the Prayers of Thanksgiving after Holy Communion, together with the troparia that follow them, then *Lord have mercy* (twelve times). *More honorable than the Cherubim..., Glory..., Both now...,* and the Lesser Dismissal: *May [He Who has risen from the dead,] Christ our true God*.... The priest then divests himself and puts his vestments away in the sacristy. Having unvested, the clergy wash their hands and, bowing to the holy table, leave the church.

CHAPTER 4

The Liturgy of the Presanctified Gifts

These directions were translated from the version published in the 2004 Богослужебные Указания (Moscow: Patriarchal Publishing House, 129ff., republished in subsequent years). A reprint of directions issued by the Holy Synod in 1916, they clarify the standard rubrics of the *Sluzhebnik*. The standard practices at Vespers and the Liturgy described earlier in this book are presumed where not directly countermanded. The editor commends these directions to the reader, not only for their considerable authority for the best practice of the prerevolutionary Russian church, but again for their relative simplicity and straightforwardness as compared with many others at present in circulation.

1. Before the Liturgy of the Presanctified Gifts, the entry prayers are said thus: at the beginning of the singing of *In Thy kingdom...,*[1] the curtain is opened, the priest and deacon leave the sanctuary by the side doors and come before the holy doors, and, making three bows from the waist before them, pray the normal beginning prayers. Then before the icon of the Savior, saying the troparion *We venerate Thy most pure icon...,* they bow down twice to the ground (thus says the Typikon; according to present established practice, the bows are made only from the waist), they kiss the icon and make a third bow to the ground. In the same way, they bow

before and kiss the icon of the Mother of God, saying the troparion: *As a fountain of tenderness....* They also venerate and kiss the icons of the church and of the feast (if there is one). (One of the prayers that is part of the complex of prayers before the full liturgy is omitted: *O Lord, stretch forth Thy hand...* in which the Lord is invoked to assist in celebrating the bloodless sacrifice.)

2. Having bowed before the holy icons, the priest and deacon, standing before the holy doors, read *Forgive, remit...,* and make one bow to the ground. Then, turning to the people, bowing from the waist and imploring pardon, they go into the sanctuary with the prayer *I will enter Thy house....* On entering the sanctuary, the celebrants bow twice to the ground before the holy table; kiss the table, the cross upon it, and the Gospel; and, having made a third bow, they bow to one another, and then robe themselves in the holy vestments.

3. The vesting prayers are not read. The priest blesses with his hand each of the vestments, kissing the cross upon each one and saying quietly: *Let us pray to the Lord.* The dismissal prayer of the Typika is said on the solea before the holy doors, and after it the priest returns to the sanctuary.

4. The priest and the deacon make three lesser bows before the holy table, praying: *God, cleanse me a sinner.* The deacon silently takes a blessing from the priest, goes out of the north door onto the solea and, prayerfully, says aloud: *Master, give the blessing.* The priest, standing before the holy table and making a sign of the cross with the Gospel book, says the opening exclamation: *Blessed is the Kingdom....* The singers: *Amen.* The reader: *O come let us worship...* and Psalm 103.

5. While the psalm is being read, the priest reads the Prayers of Light with bared head before the holy doors, beginning with the fourth *O Thou Who with never-silent*

hymns.... The first three prayers are not read here, as they will be said later, at the Short Litanies after each antiphon, while the eighteenth kathisma is being read.

6. When the psalm is completed, the Great Litany is read. The people chant *Lord, have mercy* in the Lenten tone. Kathisma eighteen follows. A peculiarity of this service is that after each antiphon of the kathisma at the vesperal Liturgy of the Presanctified Gifts, there is a Short Litany.

7. During the First Antiphon, the priest moves the Gospel book from where it lies on the holy antimension to the right of the table.[2] He then unfolds the antimension and places the paten upon it, and opens the pyx that stands upon the high place of the table. Then, having made a bow to the ground with the deacon, he reverently places the presanctified Lamb[3] upon the discos (with the spoon and the lance), after which he makes a bow to the ground. At this time, the reader concludes the First Antiphon: *Glory*.... *Both now*..., *Alleluia, Alleluia, Alleluia, glory be to Thee, O God* (three times). The deacon says the Small Litany, and the priest, in the sanctuary, reads (quietly) the Prayer of the First Antiphon (the first Prayer of Light): *O Lord compassionate and merciful*.... At the end of the litany, the priest exclaims aloud: *For Thine is the dominion*.... People: *Amen.*

8. The reader begins the Second Antiphon of the kathisma. During the Second Antiphon, the Holy Lamb is censed from around the holy table. After the exclamation *For Thine is the dominion*..., the priest and deacon make a bow to the ground before the Holy Gifts. Then the priest with the censer and the deacon with a candle go around the holy table three times, censing. At the end of the censing, both make another bow to the ground before the Holy Gifts. The deacon pronounces the Small Litany, and the priest reads (quietly) the Prayer of the Second Antiphon (the second Prayer of Light): *O Lord, rebuke us not*.... At the

end of the litany, the priest says aloud *For Thou, O God, art good*.... The people: *Amen.*

9. The reader begins the Third Antiphon of the kathisma. During the reading of the third antiphon, the Holy Lamb is transferred to the table of preparation. The priest makes a bow to the ground before the Holy Gifts, then, holding the paten close to his brow, and preceded by the deacon with a light in his left hand and the censer in his right, he carries the paten to the table of preparation, going by way of the high place. During this, all those praying within the sanctuary kneel (according to a laudable custom, those praying in the church during the reading of Third Antiphon do the same). At the table of preparation, the priest pours wine with water into the chalice, censes first the star, and places it upon the paten. He then censes the small veils, covering the paten and chalice with them as normal. After this, taking the aër, he covers the paten and chalice with it. He does not say the Prayer of the Prothesis. At each sacred censing, the priest says only: *Let us pray to the Lord; Lord, have mercy.* After having covered the holy vessels with the aër, he says: *Through the prayers of our holy fathers*.... The deacon places a lighted candle on the table of preparation before the Holy Gifts and says *Amen.* The priest censes the Holy Gifts and makes a bow to the ground.

10. After the transfer of the Holy Gifts to the table of preparation, the deacon says the Small Litany while the priest returns to the holy table, folds up the antimension, and again places the Gospel book on it, reading (quietly) the Prayer of the Third Antiphon (the third prayer of light): *O Lord our God*.... After the litany has ended, the priest says aloud: *For Thou art our God*.... The people: *Amen.*

11. *Lord, I have cried* is sung after the kathisma. There are stichera on ten verses: normally seven from the Triodion and three from the Menaion (see the relevant books for

detailed and alternative directions); *Glory be...* and sticheron if appointed; *Both now...;* Theotokion. During the singing of psalms and stichera, the entire church is censed.

12. At the last sticheron on *Both now...,* the holy doors are opened and the entry made with the censer. If there is to be a reading from the Gospels at the Liturgy of the Presanctified Gifts (for example, February 24, March 9, on the feast of the church's dedication, on a Polyeleos rank feast, or on the first three days of Holy Week), this Entrance is made with the Gospel book.

13. Deacon: *Wisdom! Let us attend.* People: *O Jesus Christ, Thou gentle light.* The prokeimenon (according to the normal order) and the reading of the first lesson (the holy doors are closed). At the end of the lesson, the deacon: *Let us attend,* the holy doors are opened. The second prokeimenon is sung. When it is completed, the deacon says aloud: *Command.* The priest, taking the censer and a candlestick with a lighted candle in both hands, stands facing the table, makes with them a sign of the cross over the Gospel book and proclaims aloud: *Wisdom! Let us attend.* After this, he turns to the west, toward the people, lifts up the candle with the censer, and says aloud: *The Light of Christ illumines all.*[4] Reader: *A reading from Proverbs.* Deacon: *Let us attend.* The holy doors are closed.

14. After the reading of the lessons has finished, the holy doors are opened. The priest, blessing the reader, says: *Peace be with thee.* The deacon: *Wisdom!* And there follow the verses of the great prokeimenon: *Let my prayer be set forth....*

[NB: *Let my prayer* is the ancient great prokeimenon of the solemn Lenten services. According to the Typikon, the reader is directed, so as to distinguish it from the prokeimena of the lessons, not to chant, but to sing it (following the normal directions given for all great prokeimena).]

15. The reader sings in the center of the church, before the ambo,[5] the appointed verses of Psalm 140: *Let my prayer....* During this, the faithful kneel, remaining thus until the end of all four verses. The singers of the choir, at the end of the reader's singing of the first verse, get up from their knees and sing: *Let my prayer...* and then kneel down again. The reader always kneels while the choir sings. The same order is followed by the reader for the other three verses: *Lord I have cried..., Set a watch...,* and *Incline not....* The singers, after each of these, sing: *Let my prayer....* When the reader sings the first half of the prokeimenon: *Let my prayer... as incense,* all get up from their knees, and the singers sing loudly: *And let... an evening sacrifice.*

16. During the verses, the priest stands (and all priests celebrating together also stand) before the table censing.[6] At the singing of the last verse: *Incline not my heart...,* the priest goes to the table of preparation and censes before it. He then gives the censer to the deacon and, reverently bowing before the holy things (a bow from the waist), he goes back to the table. Until the end of the singing of *Let my prayer...,* the presiding priest kneels down before the table, but the deacon continues to cense the Holy Gifts until the singing is finished.

17. When the singing of *Let my prayer...* has finished, the priest says the Prayer of St Ephrem (with three great prostrations). Straight after this prayer: the prokeimenon, Epistle, alleluia verses, and Gospel, if these are appointed by the Typikon. If there is no Epistle and Gospel, the holy doors are closed.

18. Litany: *Let us all say...,* and the remainder of the Liturgy of the Presanctified Gifts follows. [The litanies follow the same order as at the normal liturgy, but that for the departed is not said, and from the Wednesday of the fourth

week of Lent, the Litany for those who are preparing for Illumination is also inserted. —Ed]

19. When the singing of *Now the powers of heaven*... begins, the holy doors are opened. The deacon censes the holy sanctuary and also the priests and deacons. The iconostasis and the congregation are not censed. The deacon reads Psalm 50 quietly while censing. Then the priest, standing with the deacon before the holy table, lifts his hands on high, and prays: *Now the powers of heaven*... (three times) and kisses the holy table.

20. After that, he goes to the table of preparation, bows three times with the words: *O God, cleanse me a sinner,* censes the Holy Gifts three times and, giving the censer to the deacon, places the aër on the latter's shoulder. Then with his right hand, he takes the paten and lifts it to the level of his brow, and in the left hand he takes the chalice[7] (holding it before the breast). Thus, he takes the Holy Gifts from the table of preparation to the holy table, going out of the north door and entering the sanctuary by the holy doors. The deacon precedes the priest, facing the Holy Gifts, censing frequently as he goes[8] (the candle bearers go before the deacon, as at a full liturgy). No break at all is to be made upon the solea, and no commemorations are made.

21. As the priest begins to go in procession, all those in the church cast themselves down in prostration. Having made the Entrance, the priest places the Holy Gifts upon the antimension. The congregation stands, the people sing: *With faith and love let us draw near.* The priest takes off the small veils, places the aër (having censed it) over the Holy Gifts, and censes them. At these holy acts, nothing is said. The deacon silently takes a blessing from the priest.

22. After the singing of *With faith and love*..., the priest pronounces (at the altar) the Prayer of St Ephrem with the

three great bows. The holy doors are closed, and the curtain is closed halfway. The deacon pronounces the litany *Let us complete our evening prayer to the Lord.* Exclamation: *And count us worthy, O Master.* ... The people: *Our Father.* ... Priest: *For Thine is the kingdom* .... People: *Amen.*

23. Priest: *Peace be with you all.* People: *And with thy spirit.* Deacon: *Let us bow our heads to the Lord.* People: *To Thee, O Lord.* Priest: *Through the grace and compassion.* ... People: *Amen* (protracted). The curtain of the holy doors is closed fully. Deacon: *Let us attend.* The priest puts his right hand under the aër, reverently touches the Holy Lamb, and says aloud: *The presanctified holy things for the holy.* The people: *One is holy.* .. and the communion verse: *O taste and see that the Lord is good, Alleluia* (three times). If the Epistle and Gospel of a saint have been read, then the communion verse of the saint is sung as well.

24. The priest takes off the aër and removes the asterisk. The deacon enters the sanctuary and says: *Master, divide the Holy Bread.* The priest: *Broken and distributed.* ... He breaks the Holy Lamb and places a particle in the chalice, saying nothing. The hot water is poured into the chalice, also in silence. The priest and deacon communicate in the order given in the *Sluzhebnik* for the Liturgy of the Presanctified Gifts. (It should be noted in particular about communion, that if the Liturgy of the Presanctified Gifts is served by a priest and a deacon, then the deacon, having taken a portion of the holy supper, does not drink from the chalice or take antidoron, because he is to carry out the consumption of the Holy Gifts. The same is done by the priest, if he serves without a deacon.[9])

25. At the opening of the holy doors, the deacon says aloud: *With fear of God.* ... People: *I will bless the Lord at all times.* ... The communion of the people is carried out according to the normal order.[10]

26. The priest: *O God, save Thy people*.... The people: *Taste the heavenly bread*.... Before returning them to the table of preparation, the priest incenses the Holy Gifts three times, but the words *Be Thou exalted, O God*... are not said.[11]

27. After the priest's exclamation *Always, now and for ever*.... People: *Amen. Let our mouths be filled*.... The Prayer behind the Ambo, *O Master Almighty,* is said. People: *Amen. Blessed be the Name of the Lord*... (three times) and Psalm 33. During the reading or singing of Psalm 33, the priest gives the antidoron (kept from Sunday) to all the faithful.

28. Then the priest, blessing the people, says: *The blessing of the Lord be upon you*.... People: *Amen.* The priest: *Glory to Thee, O Christ our God*.... The people: *Glory..., Both now..., Lord, have mercy* (three times), *Give the blessing.* The dismissal is of the weekday, making a remembrance of the saints whose day it is, and also the compiler of the order of the presanctified gifts, St Gregory of the Dialogues, Pope of Rome. The people sing the Many Years: *To our great Lord and Father*....

[NB: The Typikon decrees the days on which one may serve the Liturgy of the Presanctified Gifts. These are Wednesday and Friday of the first six weeks of the Great Fast; the Thursday of the fifth week; Monday, Tuesday, and Wednesday of Holy Week; February 24 and March 9, the feast of the church's dedication, or a Polyeleos rank feast (if served on a weekday—not on a Saturday or Sunday). The celebration of the Liturgy of the Presanctified Gifts on other occasions, for example at the burial or remembrance of the departed, would be an unacceptable and incorrect interpretation of the Typikon, inasmuch as it has no major or genuine commemoration of them; lacking as it does any placing of particles in remembrance of the dead into the Blood of Christ. There are further reasons why the Liturgy of the

Presanctified Gifts cannot be served for the dead: The order has no place for the Litany of the Departed and in conjunction with this, nor is there any chant for the departed (except for vesperal stichera on *Lord, I have cried*... on the Fridays of the second, third, and fourth weeks, because the Saturdays of these weeks are for commemorating the departed). From this, it follows that the Liturgy of the Presanctified Gifts is not celebrated on any other days than those that are decreed by the Typikon.[12]

The practice described here is that of the contemporary Russian church and is the same as that laid down by the *Sluzhebnik* and in the liturgical books produced by the Orthodox Church in America (*Service Books of the Orthodox Church*, Volume 2 (South Canaan, PA: St Tikhon's Press, 1984), 155–6. By contrast, a typical modern Greek *Hieratikon* (Athens: Apostolike Diakonia, 1992) 218, requires the formula *The fullness of the Holy Spirit* to be said when the portion $I\Sigma$ is placed in the chalice, and the rubrics expect the priest and deacon to receive communion in the normal way. The "fullness" formula is also found in other and older sources, e.g., the Moghila *Sluzhebnik* of 1639 (reprinted Lvov and Fairfax, VA, 1996, 662ff.). This book, often thought to be a Latinizing work, expects both priest and deacon to receive from the chalice with the usual formula referring to the Precious Blood. These two examples witness to the older tradition that saw the chalice as having been consecrated by contact with the presanctified Lamb. The Latin influence that led to the present Russian practice is therefore of late date and should probably not be regarded as doctrinally binding. The editor would, however, counsel clergy considering change to not do so without asking the blessing of their bishops. The contemporary unwillingness in the Russian church to communicate infants at this service stems from the same understanding.

The Kiev Caves Monastery was in the habit of celebrating the presanctified daily, Monday to Friday, excepting only the Monday and Tuesday of the first week (see Fr K. Nikolsky, *Uchebnyj Ustav Bogosluzheniya* [reprinted Moscow: 1999], 476, footnote 1). The present practice of the monastery is not known to the editor.]

Vestment Colors

As is well known, the Roman Catholic Church and other Western churches have a clearly defined scheme for deciding the colors of the vestments to be worn throughout the year, and this scheme is often printed in liturgical calendars. It is often widely assumed that the Orthodox Church has no such scheme, other than that white or other bright vestments are worn for feasts, and dark vestments for fasting periods, especially for Lent (and in some cases for funerals). It is less well known that the Roman scheme, now widely used throughout Western churches, is only datable to about the sixteenth century and that a systematic scheme has been in use in Russia since at least the nineteenth century. Eastern rite Catholic groups such as the Ukrainian and Carpatho-Rusyn Greek Catholics have had such schemes for some time, no doubt in imitation of the Roman Catholic ones.

The scheme that follows (from the 2006 *Bogosluzhebniya Ukazaniya*) does seem to accord with the editor's experience in Russia and seems to be largely followed in Ukraine and Belarus as well. It is provided as a guide rather than a supposedly strict rule (no Orthodox calendar known to the editor prints indications as to color). Many churches in the English-speaking world possess only white, gold, and, perhaps, red vestments. At the very least, a church should probably possess light festal vestments for Sundays and feasts and dark vestments for Lent and other occasions such as feasts of the cross. Two additional points might be made, however. Sunday is always the feast of the Resurrection and so, even in Lent, black vestments are never suggested for Sunday in any of the known schemes. Secondly, although Gaslov does suggest dark vestments for funerals, common practice recently has been to revert to the white of primitive Christianity. Black vestments were unknown to the Russian church in ancient times and appear only to have been used from the time of the funeral of the Emperor Peter II in 1730. However, a series of popular prints of the funeral of Emperor Alexander III in 1894 show the clergy in white.

The Color of the Vestments for Divine Service[1]

Nativity of the Most Holy Mother of God (until leave-taking inclusive)	Light blue
Exaltation of the Holy Cross (until leave-taking inclusive) and the other feasts in honor of the Cross of the Lord	Claret[2] or violet
The Holy Apostle and Evangelist St John the Theologian	White
Protection of the Most Holy Mother of God Entry into the Temple of the Most Holy Mother of God (until leave-taking inclusive)	Light blue
Eve of the Nativity of Christ	White
The Nativity of Christ (until leave-taking inclusive)	Gold or white
Synaxis of the Most Holy Mother of God	White or light blue
Circumcision of the Lord Eve of Theophany Theophany (Baptism of the Lord) (until leave-taking inclusive)	White
The Meeting of the Lord (until leave-taking inclusive)	Light blue or white

The Color of the Vestments for Divine Service *(continued)*

The Annunciation to the Most Holy Mother of God	Light blue
Sundays of preparation for the Great Fast	Violet or gold (yellow)
Great Fast (weekdays)	Violet, crimson, or black[3]
Saturdays and Sundays of the Great Fast and Polyeleos rank feasts on the weekdays of the Great Fast	Violet
Liturgy of the Presanctified Gifts	Violet, crimson, or black
Sunday of the Veneration of the Cross	Violet or claret
Entry of the Lord into Jerusalem	Green or white
Holy Week	Black or dark violet
Great Thursday	Violet[4]
Great Saturday (in the liturgy, after the reading of the Epistle) and from the beginning of the service of Holy Pascha (until the end of Matins of the first day of Pascha)	White
Pascha (until the leave-taking inclusive)	Red[5]
Ascension of the Lord (until leave-taking inclusive)	White
Pentecost (Trinity Sunday) (until leave-taking inclusive)	Green
Monday of the Holy Spirit	Green or white
Nativity of St John the Forerunner	White
Holy First Apostles Peter and Paul	Gold (yellow) or white
Transfiguration of the Lord (until leave-taking inclusive)	White
Falling Asleep of the Most Holy Mother of God (until leave-taking inclusive)[6]	Light blue
Beheading of St John the Forerunner	Red or claret
Lesser feasts of the Lord on weekdays and Sundays outside of the Great Fast	Gold (yellow)
Feasts of the Mother of God	Light blue
Commemorations of the Bodiless Powers,[7] Holy Women and Virgins	White

The Color of the Vestments for Divine Service *(continued)*

Commemorations of Prophets	Gold (yellow) or white
Commemorations of Apostles	Gold (yellow), white, or red
Commemorations of Male Saints	Gold (yellow)
Commemorations of Martyrs	Red
Commemorations of Ascetics and Fools for Christ's Sake	Green
Commemorations of Holy Princes	Gold (yellow), green, or red[8]
Services for the Departed (outside of the Great Fast)	White
The Mystery of Baptism	White
The Mystery of Marriage	White, gold, or red (from Thomas Sunday to the leave-taking of Pascha)

Gaslov's directions are similar but less detailed. He directs gold, red, or other colors at the discretion of the Rector on Sundays and feasts of the Lord. The differences from the above table are that a darker blue may substitute for violet on the Exaltation of the Cross, at the Vigil of the Procession of the Cross (August 1/14), and on the Sunday of the Veneration of the Cross.

White may be substituted for light blue on feasts of the Mother of God. White is also worn for Processions to the Blessing of Water (on Theophany, Mid-Pentecost, and the Liturgy of August 1/14), and at the liturgy on Holy Thursday.

He suggests only red for Apostles, and black or dark vestments for the Great Fast and services for the departed.

A Complete Collection of Canon Responses[1]

I. THE REFRAINS OF THE SUNDAY AND WEEKDAY CANONS

The canon of the Resurrection: *Glory to Thy holy Resurrection, O Lord.*

The canon of the Cross and Resurrection: *Glory to Thy precious Cross, and Thy Resurrection, O Lord.*

The Sunday canon and all other canons to the Mother of God: *Most Holy Mother of God, save us.*

The Bodiless Powers: *Holy Archangels and Angels, pray to God for us.*

John the Forerunner: *Holy great John the Forerunner and Baptist of the Lord, pray to God for us.*

The precious Cross: *Glory to Thy precious Cross, O Lord.*

The Apostles: *Holy Apostles, pray to God for us.*

St Nicholas the Wonderworker: *Holy Father Nicholas, pray to God for us.*

All Saints: *All you Saints, pray to God for us.*

Canon for the Departed: *Give rest, O Lord, to the souls of your departed servants.*

II. GENERAL REFRAINS

A prophet: *Holy Prophet N, pray to God for us.*

An apostle: *Holy Apostle N, pray to God for us.*

Or: *Apostle of Christ N, pray to God for us.*

Two or more apostles: *Holy Apostles, pray to God for us.*

A male saint: *Holy father N, pray to God for us.*

Several saints in general: *Holy great saints, pray to God for us.*

A monastic or master of the ascetic life: *Venerable Father N, pray to God for us.*

Two or more monastics: *Venerable Father, pray to God for us.*

A martyr: *Holy Martyr N, pray to God for us.*

Martyrs in general: *Holy Martyrs, pray to God for us.*

A hieromartyr: *Holy Hieromartyr N, pray to God for us.*
  Or: *Hieromartyr and Father N, pray to God for us.*

Hieromartyrs in general: *Holy Hieromartyrs, pray to God for us.*

A monastic martyr: *Holy venerable Martyr N, pray to God for us.*

Several monastic martyrs: *Holy venerable Martyrs, pray to God for us.*

A monastic confessor:[2] *Venerable Father and Confessor N, pray to God for us.*

A hiero-confessor: *Holy in Christ and Confessor N, pray to God for us.*

Hieromartyr and confessor: *Holy Hieromartyr and Confessor N, pray to God for us.*

Several martyrs and confessors: *Holy Martyrs and Confessors N, pray to God for us.*

A new martyr: *Holy new Martyr N, pray to God for us.*

Several Russian new martyrs: *New Martyrs of Russia, pray to God for us.*

A holy and righteous prince: *Holy righteous prince N, pray to God for us.*

Several princes: *Holy righteous princes N and N, pray to God for us.*

A passion-bearing prince: *Holy Passion-Bearer prince N, pray to God for us.*

Several passion-bearing princes: *Holy Passion-Bearing princes N and N, pray to God for us.*

Unmercenary saints: *Holy wonderworkers and unmercenaries N and N, pray to God for us.*

A blessed Fool for Christ: *Holy blessed N, pray to God for us.*

A female martyr: *Holy Martyr N, pray to God for us.*
  Or: *Holy Great Martyr N, pray to God for us.*

Two or more female martyrs: *Holy Martyrs, pray to God for us.*

A female monastic or ascetic: *Venerable Mother N, pray to God for us.*

Several female monastics: *Holy Venerable Mothers, pray to God for us.*
  Or: *Holy and Venerable women, pray to God for us.*

A nun-martyr: *Holy Venerable Martyr N, pray to God for us.*

A righteous woman: *Holy Righteous N, pray to God for us.*

A righteous princess: *Holy Righteous Princess N, pray to God for us.*

III. SOME ADDITIONAL REFRAINS

New Year, Feasts of the Lord, canons of the Holy Trinity: *Glory be to Thee, our God, glory be to Thee.*

Canons of the Holy Trinity: *All-Holy Trinity, our God, glory to Thee.*

The Archangel Michael: *Holy Archangel Michael, pray to God for us.*

Feasts of the Mother of God and of Icons of the Mother of God: *Most Holy Mother of God, save us.*

An apostle and evangelist: *Holy Apostle and Evangelist N, pray to God for us.*

A first martyr: *Holy First Martyr N, pray to God for us.*

The seven sleepers of Ephesus: *Holy Martyrs, pray to God for us.*

Or: *Holy Seven Young Men, pray to God for us.*

The three children [i.e., Shadrach, Meshach, and Abednego. —Ed.]: *Holy Three Children, pray to God for us.*

The assembly of the Forefathers: *Holy Forefathers, pray to God for us.*

The assembly of the Fathers: *Holy Fathers, pray to God for us.*

On the Sunday after the Nativity of Christ: *Holy Ancestors of God, pray to God for us.*

Notes for Concelebration by Priests in the Absence of a Bishop

It is common in the United States and the United Kingdom for Orthodox clergy to concelebrate even when the bishop is not present, but for some clergy these are rare events that are almost as nerve wracking as a hierarchical liturgy. The chapter on the liturgy in this book does give some guidance on how to concelebrate, especially in the absence of a deacon, but a few more points may be worth bearing in mind.

1. Priests concelebrate as sharers in an act of worship and not as a demonstration of clerical privilege. The main celebrant and the deacon, if one is present, should be the clear leaders of the liturgical assembly. Concelebrants are present as fellow worshippers and not as competitors.

2. In churches that observe strict seniority by rank, the most senior priest in rank present should preside. Such a priest, if present simply as a visitor, will cede presidency to the Rector of the parish. The same applies where seniority is determined only by years of ordination. If a monk and a married priest serve together who are of equal rank or age (according to the local custom), the monk is senior.

3. The priests are always fully vested and stand at the altar in the order of their seniority, just as when the bishop serves.

4. Concelebrants stand at the sides of the altar, facing across it. They must not stand behind or in front of the altar,

and if there are a large number, they form a second rank behind the first.

5. The concelebrants should, wherever possible, leave enough room for the deacon or another concelebrant to pass in front of them. Servers should pass behind the priests.

6. Concelebrants should have small liturgical books that they can place in a pocket or on a nearby table when not needed. They should not place their books on the altar at any time.

7. The chief celebrant bows to each in turn of seniority to indicate that they should take an ekphonesis (or a litany when there is no deacon). At the ekphonesis, the priest reading turns to the east and bows when naming the persons of the Trinity and then turns back and bows to the chief celebrant.

8. As a general rule, concelebrating clergy read quietly all prayers that they cannot hear the chief celebrant say; otherwise, they listen prayerfully.

9. Litanies are shared out among the priests only when no deacon is present, and a single litany should not be divided among different priests as this makes for a confusing effect for the other worshippers.

10. At the Little Entrance, the priests follow the deacon carrying the Gospel book, junior concelebrant first and chief celebrant coming last. On the solea, they stand in exactly the same order as they did in the sanctuary, forming two lines facing east, the chief celebrant and deacon standing at the west end of the two lines. When all are in position, they bow together to the east, turn and bow to the celebrant, and face each other.[1] After the priest has blessed the Entrance and kissed the Gospel book,[2] the deacon goes forward with the Gospel book and says *Wisdom, Let us stand aright* and enters the sanctuary. If there is no deacon, the chief celebrant remains at the outer (west end) of the ranks of other

clergy for *Wisdom, Let us stand aright*. In either case, the concelebrants first turn to bow to the chief celebrant and then turn east and enter the sanctuary, kissing the small icon on whatever side they are on, and resume their positions at the altar. When the chief celebrant is ready to kiss the altar, all the concelebrants do likewise.

11. At *Glory be*... of the Trisagion, the chief celebrant bows and kisses the altar (the others do likewise) and goes to the high place, passing in front of the right-hand rank of clergy. As he passes the other clergy from the senior onward, both sides follow him so that at the high place, the most senior will stand to the chief celebrant's left and the next to his right (across the bishop's seat), and so on.

12. The chief celebrant may ask a concelebrant to give the greeting *Peace be with you all*.

13. The priests should sit during the Apostle but stand when the deacon comes to incense them in order of seniority.

14. At the Alleluia, the chief celebrant goes to give the Gospel book to the deacon (with the blessing, if that is the custom) and returns to the high place. If there is no deacon, he goes to read the Gospel, and in either case, the concelebrants remain standing in the high place.

15. After the Gospel (and sermon, if preached here), led by the most senior, the concelebrants return to either side of the altar.

16. During the ektene, the two most senior concelebrants unfold the iliton and the bottom of the antimension, if this is the custom and may be done without fuss.

17. At *Open to them the Gospel*, the next two concelebrants may fully open the antimension.

18. The sponge is kissed only by the chief celebrant.

19. At the Great Entrance, the chief celebrant *may* share the saying of the Cherubic Hymn with two concelebrants in turn.

20. When the chief celebrant has bowed to ask the prayers of the concelebrants and the people, the concelebrants, two by two, come in front of the altar, bow twice, kiss the antimension and the edge of the altar, bow once more, and then bow to each other and finally to the people. They then go and line up in order behind the chief celebrant, picking up a cross to carry in procession. The most junior does not pick up a cross but carries the lance and spoon crossed.

21. The procession is led by the deacon with the chalice and the chief celebrant with the discos; the others follow, most senior first, junior last. When the chief celebrant has reached the holy doors and turns to face the people, the concelebrants stop and do likewise. If there are a large number of concelebrants, they form another rank behind the first on the solea. This means that the concelebrants form ranks facing the worshippers on one side only and do not have to try and go around the chief celebrant, possibly causing confusion.

22. There is no need for every concelebrant to make a commemoration aloud, when the chief celebrant says finally, *You and all Orthodox Christians...,* they all make the sign of the cross over the people with whatever they are holding and say quietly to one another *May the Lord remember your priesthood in his kingdom...,* as they follow the chief celebrant into the sanctuary, without kissing the small icons on the sides of the doors.

23. Up to two crosses are placed on the altar; the rest are returned to the sacristan, and the lance and spoon are placed on either side of the cross on the right side of the chief celebrant, lance to the left and spoon to the right (thus on the right and left sides of the figure of Christ). The concelebrants otherwise resume their positions with as little fuss as possible.

24. In some places, it is customary (when there is no deacon) for a second celebrant to take the second part of the Litany of Supplication, from *Help us, save us*... to the end, in order to allow time for all to say the prayer. This might be repeated at the same litany before the *Our Father*.

25. At the sign of peace, the senior concelebrant leaves his place and, passing around the rear of the altar, leads the others to the left side in time for the chief celebrant to finish kissing the Gifts. He bows and then comes and kisses the Gifts himself and turns to receive the greeting of peace from the chief celebrant. The others follow in order.

26. The chief celebrant, and then each other celebrant, greets the one coming to him with *Christ is in our midst;* the other responds *He is and shall be,* and they kiss each other's right and left shoulders and the backs of their right hands. Where it is customary, they kiss the cheek. Non-concelebrating priests do not take part in the exchange, and deacons exchange the peace only with each other on the solea.

27. As they finish exchanging the peace, the priests assist the chief celebrant in gently waving the aër up and down over the Gifts. When it is taken away from the Gifts, they may kiss the edge of the aër if convenient, and one of the concelebrants may fold it and put it in its place.

28. The chief celebrant alone leads the dialogue that begins the Anaphora and alone lifts up the hands at *Let us lift up our hearts*. All the celebrants bow at *Let us give thanks to the Lord*.

29. When the deacon (or chief celebrant in his absence) removes the star, he kisses it and places it down. Nobody else kisses it.

30. According to the rubrics of the *Chinovnik*,[3] the words *Take, eat* and *Drink from this, all of you*... are said quietly by all the concelebrants, who should synchronize their words with those of the chief celebrant, neither preceding nor

following him. They are to do the same at the words *And make this bread...* and so on, at the Epiklesis. In both cases, only the chief celebrant makes the gestures with the hand required by the rubrics.

31. The chief celebrant may share out the saying of *O Lord, Who at the third hour* with two other celebrants, as at the Great Entrance.

32. Having broken the Lamb and placed the particle **IC** in the chalice and the deacon having poured in the hot water, the chief celebrant cuts the particle **XC** into sufficient small particles for each concelebrant, deacon, and any other clergy who are to receive Holy Communion. While he is doing this, the senior concelebrant again leads the others around the back of the altar and waits to the left of the chief celebrant.

33. When the chief celebrant has finished cutting the particle **XC** he stands back a little so that the concelebrants, senior first, may come forward to take a particle for their own communion. Each approaches from the left and kisses the altar, saying *The precious and most holy...* and with the fingers of the left hand takes a particle and places it in the right hand; he then covers the particle with the left hand and, if it is the custom, exchanges the Kiss of Peace with the chief celebrant. He then returns to his original place, turning to his left and passing in front of the other concelebrants. He then waits there with his hands on the holy table.

34. Other non-concelebrating priests follow the concelebrants, wearing stole, cuffs, and chasuble. After the priests have taken their particles, the chief celebrant distributes to the deacon or deacons, takes a particle for himself and, placing his hands upon the table, says (in a manner audible to all the clergy) *I believe, O Lord...* and all receive.

35. The chief celebrant receives from the chalice and may pass the cloth to the senior celebrant. He then moves

to the left and may commence cutting particles for the communion of the people. The senior concelebrant comes forward and receives communion from the chalice and, having passed the cloth to the next priest, simply stands back. All the celebrants approach from the right side, and after any non-concelebrating priests, the last concelebrant ministers the chalice to the deacon.

36. The chief celebrant may designate one of the concelebrants to consume the Holy Gifts in the absence of a deacon (usually he who served the Proskomedia), and all the others receive *zapivka,* having first said quietly the prayer: *We thank Thee, O Master....*

37. During the communion of the faithful, the priests remain quietly in the sanctuary and may read the Prayers of Thanksgiving after Holy Communion. If required, some may assist with communion, either with another chalice or in wiping the communicants' lips with the communion cloth.

38. If there is no deacon, the chief celebrant takes both discos and chalice back to the table of preparation. As he does so, the senior concelebrant may fold the antimension and iliton, and put the Gospel book upright upon them.

39. The junior concelebrant says the Prayer behind the Ambo, having first bowed to the chief celebrant, kissed the altar, and said *Let us go forth in peace.* If he is to consume the Holy Gifts, he returns to the table of preparation directly and says the prayer *Christ our God, Who art Thyself the fulfillment...,* and begins to consume the gifts.

40. The other concelebrants remain in their places while the chief concelebrant concludes the liturgy. If the sermon is preached at the end, it is customary for the priests to stand on the solea while it is delivered. If there are a very great number of faithful, the chief celebrant may ask one or more other priests to assist in giving the holy cross.

NOTES

Introduction

1. I. V. Gaslov, *Pravoslavnoe Bogosluzhenie: Prakticheskoye Rukovodstvo dlya Klirikov i Miryan* [*Orthodox Divine Service: A Practical Handbook for Clergy and Laity*] (St Petersburg: Satis, 1998).

Chapter 1: Little Vespers and the All-Night Vigil

1. In Russia at 3:00 p.m. to 4:00 p.m.in the winter, 5:00 p.m. in the summer.

2. The Typikon lists the following chimes: (a) Festal, (b) Sunday, (c) Polyeleos, (d) daily, (e) little, and (f) *zazvonnye*; the little bells are used in the ringing of the *Trezvon* or peal.

3. The Russian service books know of no order of prayers to be observed when entering the church and sanctuary in order to celebrate the evening services. Nor do they say anything about the vesting, which simply follows the standard tradition of that place. There is a tradition derived from the Greek service books and imitated from Greek practice by many Russian priests: The celebrating priest, going to church, stands on the ambo before the holy doors, makes three bows to the sanctuary, and then turns around to the people and bows once, saying: *Forgive and bless, fathers and mothers, brothers and sisters.* He then enters the sanctuary by the south door, saying the prayer: *I will*

enter Thine house.... Going into the sanctuary, he makes
a prostration to the ground before the altar and kisses the
Gospel book and the edge of the altar.

4. According to the universal practice of the Russian
Orthodox Church, when celebrating Little Vespers the
priest not only wears the stole but also the cuffs. The
Russian service books are silent about any vesting prayers
at Vespers; the Greek service books decree the following
order: Making three bows to the high place, the priest
takes the stole in his left hand and blesses it with his right,
saying: *Blessed be our God, always now and ever and to the
ages of ages. Amen.* And, kissing the cross on the top of the
stole, places it upon himself saying the following prayer:
Blessed be God Who has poured out... as at the liturgy.
Analogously, he then takes the cuffs in the same way and
says the prayers: *Thy right hand*... and *Thy hands have made
me and fashioned me...,* while putting on the cuffs.

5. The first and ninth chapters of the Typikon require
the reading of the Ninth Hour in the narthex or in the
church, but on the following fasting days—first day of
the Nativity Fast 15/28 November and the Monday of the
first week of the Great Fast—it decrees the reading of the
Ninth Hour in the church.

6. This exclamation is rightly only made by a priest.
For lower clergy it is required (in the absence of a priest)
that they say: *Through the prayers of our holy Fathers....*

7. The first two prayers are omitted during the
season of Holy Pentecost (from Easter Sunday until Holy
Trinity) and also at the services for the departed and on the
weekdays of the Great Fast.

8. If there is no priest, this exclamation is omitted, and
the reader, without making any kind of pause, immediately
continues: *Lord, have mercy* (twelve times), *Glory..., Both
now..., O Come let us worship....*

9. "*Alleluia* (three times)" means that one reads *Alleluia, Alleluia, Alleluia: Glory to Thee, O God* three times.

10. If the appointed day is one when the festival of two saints is celebrated, or a feast and a saint and so on, the first (major) troparion is read before *Glory*... and the second, after.

11. The phrases "Trisagion to the *Our Father*" or "Trisagion Prayers" means that one reads all those prayers given in the normal beginning except the first two.

12. For the whole of the Little Vespers, the holy doors and the curtain remain closed.

13. If the Ninth Hour was not served before Little Vespers, then after the *Amen,* the reader says the usual beginning.

14. In place of the Great Litany of Great Vespers, one substitutes this in its place.

15. Or it may be read by the reader.

16. If there is no second choir, then all that is written here is sung by the one choir.

17. At Little Vespers are sung four stichera on *Lord I have cried*. These stichera are found in the order of Great Vespers in the Octoechos. The first stichera of Little Vespers answers to the first resurrection sticheron of Great Vespers, then in place of the second sticheron this one is repeated and then the third and fourth stichera answer to the second and third resurrection stichera of Great Vespers.

18. *Glory*..., *Both now*..., and the Lesser Theotokion may be sung by either choir or both together.

19. There is no Entrance at Little Vespers.

20. Without any introductory verse.

21. Longer verses are found in the order of Little Vespers in the Octoechos, but as in the services of the Mother of God.

22. Or both choirs together.

23. That is, the Lesser Dismissal.

24. That is, at what the Typikon calls the first hour of the night and is 6–7 o'clock in the evening in modern terms.

25. Psalm 118.

26. The greater part of the tradition says nothing more than this about the order of entering the church and sanctuary, nor of the vesting that precedes the services. (Greek tradition does have such an order as we saw when describing Little Vespers.)

27. In blessing the censer, he should extend his hand over the censer itself and not just the chains.

28. This practice is followed in some Russian churches and monasteries.

29. At the three swings, the censer is swung out, and once during each of the three swings, the person censing bows as the censer falls back.

30. The server does the same if he gives the censer to the priest, but not when he gives it to the deacon.

31. According to some traditions, this acclamation is sung by the people (choir).

32. If there are two choirs, the first, or chief, one responds.

33. In the eighth tone according to the Typikon, "not quickly but melodiously."

34. Various arrangements, characteristic of the Slav and Greek churches, respectively, are used to divide the verses and responses of Psalm 103.

35. In threes with bows.

36. If several choirs sing, then he begins by censing the chief (those who sing the main chants), then the remainder in descending order.

37. In another tradition, by the south side of the altar.

38. Without the phelonion (i.e., he takes it off before going out onto the solea, kissing the cross on its back, and goes on to the solea by the north door, in stole and cuffs).

39. They are correctly done according to the *obikhod* chant or that of the Kiev Caves Monastery that expands them. Otherwise, the reader reads the additional verses.

40. Before going out of the north door to read the prayers, the priest kisses the edge of the altar. Similarly, when he returns to the sanctuary by the south door after reading the prayers, he again kisses the edge of the table.

41. If the solea has a proper ambo, then the Great Litany is proclaimed there.

42. If the deacon is alone on the solea, then he makes the bows standing before the holy doors; if the priest is still standing on the solea, then the deacon makes his bows standing before the icon of the Mother of God, the priest standing at that time before the icon of the Savior.

43. Thumb, index, and middle.

44. After the Great Litany, the deacon may remain on the solea, awaiting the moment for the Small Litany that follows the first antiphon of the first kathisma.

45. *Nastolnaya Kniga Svyashchennika* (hereafter *NKS*; Lestvitsa, 1998), 5 and 37, and Archpriest Arkadii Neapolitanskii, *Tserkonvyi Ustav v Tablitsach* (hereafter *TsU*; Moscow: A. D. Stupin, n.d., reprinted Patriarchal Publishing House, 1994).

46. The first antiphon being sung in the eighth tone, and the second and the third in the tone of that Sunday.

47. In some choral traditions, the Alleluia is sung only once.

48. *NKS*; op. cit., 5.

49. If there is a canonarch, then he begins with the words: *In* such and such *tone, Lord, I have cried, Lord, hear me*.

50. One edition of the *obikhod* decrees a special chant for each tone, another one a chant for all the tones. The verses can, however, be read by the reader.

51. In some traditions, the deacon prefaces the request for the blessing with the words: *Let us pray to the Lord*.

52. Holding the stole with his left hand.

53. See *NKS*, 15.

54. If there is no canonarch, then the choir sings the first half verse.

55. To the proper chant in the tone of the sticheron.

56. The canonarch may begin the sticheron or precent each line.

57. This is as laid down in the order of the singing of the festal stichera on a Sunday of one minor saint (i.e., a saint "without a sign").

58. There may be just the one, in which case he follows the directions for the first candle bearer. According to the Typikon, the candle bearers may be two servers, or a reader and a server.

59. In some churches the candle bearers descend from the solea and stop below it before the holy doors, and they mount the solea only at the singing of *O Jesus Christ, Thou gentle Light*.

60. On finishing the prayer, the priest bows.

61. In some places, it is normal for the deacon, after the priest has entered the sanctuary, to go out to the solea again and cense those standing in the church, and then go back to the sanctuary, censing the right side of the table and the priest, by now standing at the left side of the high place.

62. The first candle bearer through the south door and the second through the north. As a rule, if they are standing on the solea, they remain there before the holy doors until the hymn is finished.

63. *NKS,* 6.

64. *TsU*, appendix, p. 2.

65. Ibid. and *TsU,* Appendix, page 2.

66. Such is still the practice in some monasteries and parish churches.

67. If the narthex is very small, then the Lity is served in the west part of the church.

68. Traditionally, the candle bearers face each other.

69. Normally, the deacon does not have time to cense the whole church, and so, after censing the sanctuary and iconostasis, he goes directly to the narthex.

70. According to the Typikon, this prayer is expected to be read facing the west.

71. The Typikon directs the singing of the Aposticha to be done by both choirs together, as they go from the narthex into the church; nowadays, the choirs do not go in procession to the narthex.

72. In the *Sluzhebnik,* he is directed to cense the priest first and then the Lity table.

73. In another tradition, there is no blessing, but as the objects are named they are touched with the fingers.

74. In another tradition, Psalm 33 is read by the reader, and in a third (found in older Typika and chant books), the reader reads the psalm, but the last verse *The rich have become poor and hungry* is sung by the people.

75. In another tradition, he stands in the holy doors.

76. If the holy doors were closed for the Lity and blessing of bread, then he goes in by the north door.

77. The behavior of the worshippers during the Six Psalms is laid down in Chapter 2 of the modern Typikon. The ancient Typika (e.g., that of 1633) clarify further: "Let the ecclesiarch chant the Six Psalms attentively in this, the usual way. Each and all must attend with reverence and diligence. Thus all will attend as if God Himself is present, while reflecting on their sinfulness. The chanting is in a clear but quiet voice that is audible to all. There must be no chattering or spitting or anything else that disturbs the peace of the church during the chanting of the Six Psalms, nor should anything else be done. No movement or sign should be made. Even if a venerable elder or someone in need should wish to go outside, none may do anything, no

matter what. All should remain like this in the church until the end of the Six Psalms and then go out if necessary."

78. In another tradition, the deacon exclaims: *The Lord is God* in front of the holy doors.

79. In another tradition, the four repetitions of *The Lord is God* are sung straight through, the first being sung at the same time as the deacon's first exclamation of *The Lord is God*.

80. *NKS*, 17, and *TsU* appendix, page 4.

81. In practice, only one kathisma is read, and just one psalm from each *stasis*.

82. If the next litany is to be omitted, then during the reading of the Sessional Hymns the holy doors are opened, and at the end of the Sessional Hymns, they begin to sing the Polyeleos.

83. *NKS*, ibid.

84. In modern practice, the Polyeleos is sung on Sundays throughout the year, although the Typikon indicates that on certain Sundays it should be replaced by Psalm 118.

85. The church Typikon is clear that in the ancient chant traditions the Polyeleos comprised all the verses of Psalms 134 and 135. In the modern musical settings, the quantity of verses is very much reduced, but no less than those directed should be sung.

86. In some musical settings, *Alleluia* is sung just once.

87. These troparia are not sung on Thomas Sunday and on feasts of the Lord that fall on a Sunday: Pascha, Pentecost, or Entry into Jerusalem.

88. So as to allow space for the censing.

89. Or the reader may read.

90. As a rule, it is not that the priest kisses the Gospel book so much as he kisses the actual passage that has been read.

91. [This is common practice, but I have not yet found an authoritative description.—Ed.]

92. In collegiate churches (sobors), the clergy kiss the Gospel after the prayer *O God, save Thy people*.... Normally, the clergy sing *We have seen*... together with the people.

93. If there is a great crowd of people, then in other parts of the church where there are further analoys for festal icons, other priests may bring and place on them small Gospel books of the type used for sacramental rites. Thus great disorder can be avoided in the venerating and kissing of the Gospel book in a way that takes up less time.

94. In another tradition, the deacon pronounces this prayer in the middle of the church.

95. If there was a Lity, then some traditions omit the reading of this prayer at Matins.

96. In some places, the deacon goes into the sanctuary.

97. Model responses to the canons may be found in Appendix 2.

98. *NKS,* 17, and S. V. Bulgakov, *Nastolnaya Kniga I* (reprinted Moscow: 1993), 869, note 33. Also Chapter 2 of the Typikon.

99. The Eirmos tune "veleglasno." In some churches, this canticle is sung together with the people.

100. *NKS,* ibid., and Bulgakov, op. cit.

101. The reader may read it.

102. That of the Sunday.

103. In some traditions, these verses are read by the reader; in others they are now omitted.

104. According to the Typikon, this and the following stichera are sung by both choirs together.

105. That of the Gospel sticheron.

106. According to an older tradition, this Theotokion was sung in the tone of the week.

107. But in actual practice, hands are lifted up.

108. [The instructions in *NKS* at this point (p. 18) direct the priest who serves without a deacon to take the last

two litanies and the prayer with bowed head on the solea, but the order in which they are described indicates that a weekday service is referred to, when the holy doors would be closed. At the Sunday and festal service, the doors are open and the litanies are taken at the altar.—Ed.]

109. Usually he only reads Psalm 100.

Chapter 2: The Third and Sixth Hours

1. As has already been mentioned, the Divine Liturgy is traditionally preceded by the service of the Third and Sixth Hours, and they are done at the same time that the Liturgy of Preparation is being carried out in the sanctuary (see the next chapter on the liturgy). During this time, the tolling of the bell for the Hours is substituted by the toll for the Divine Liturgy, although the older church Typikon decreed a particular tolling of the bell for the service of the Hours (still maintained during the Great Fast). Before the Third Hour, the *blagovest* is rung on the daily bell, and then, "by the hour," i.e., it is struck the number of times of each hour (Third, three times; Sixth, six times, and so on) on the same bell.

2. Observing the order of the Entrance into the church, and then vested in the sanctuary in stole and cuffs, according to the order laid down for that church or diocese (see the directions for these at the beginning of the order of Little Vespers and of the All-Night Vigil).

3. If at this time they are ready to carry out the Liturgy of Preparation (or are in the process of carrying it out), then the priest pronounces these words in the sanctuary standing before the holy table. If the service of the Hours is not celebrated at the time of the celebration of the Liturgy of Preparation, then he stands before the holy doors, and remains there until the exclamation *For Thine is the kingdom...,* after which he goes back into the sanctuary.

4. This may be another reader beside the one serving at all the services of the daily round, or a separate reader, designated by the Rector to read the Third (or Third and Sixth) Hours.

5. If the service is one of two (lesser) saints, then the first troparion.

6. [If a bishop is present, then: *Master, give the blessing* and the priest replies: *Through the prayers of our holy Master, O Lord Jesus Christ, have mercy on us.*—Ed.]

7. In a similar way, the "normal beginning" prayers are read only before the Third Hour.

8. If the service is one of two (lesser) saints, then the second troparion is read.

Chapter 3: The Divine Liturgy According to the Order of St John Chrysostom

1. This practice is not ordered by the *Sluzhebnik,* but is observed in the majority of the churches of Russia and the Greek East. According to the *Sluzhebnik,* the entry prayers are read before entering the sanctuary, in which case the priest does not vest in the stole. [The latter is the better practice.—*Sluzhebnik*]

2. The *Sluzhebnik* says that these troparia are read by the priest and deacon together. The Greek *Sluzhebnik* gives a different practice: The troparion *Have mercy...* is read by the priest, *Glory* and troparion *Lord, have mercy on us...* are read by the deacon, and *Both now...* and *Open to us the doors of compassion...* again by the priest.

3. In one tradition, the deacon enters through the south door and the priest through the north door; according to another, both enter through the south door.

4. From verses 8–15 of Psalm 5.

5. This prayer is lacking in the Russian books, but is found in the Greek and is used in some Russian churches following an older tradition.

6. The *Sluzhebnik* says nothing of this; the deacon, unvested, may ready the table of preparation before the entry prayers or before vesting.

7. And, if necessary, that on the holy table.

8. And, if necessary, on the holy table.

9. Checking for any imperfections, and selecting that which to be the Holy Lamb.

10. Russian service books agree in placing this prayer here.

11. In contradistinction to the other acclamations of the Liturgy of Preparation, this acclamation may be uttered aloud by the priest when it also serves to begin the Third Hour.

12. A larger one may be used if necessary.

13. Only a small amount of water is mixed in, so as not to destroy the taste of the wine.

14. [The blessing given in some books is not found in the *Sluzhebnik*.—Ed.]

15. The pouring should not be too precipitate, especially in summer, and he should first glance into the chalice to ensure that there are no insects in it.

16. In one tradition, this is a normal prosphora, marked with the sign of the cross and the letters **IC, XC, NI,** and **KA**. In another tradition, it is a special Mother of God prosphora with an image of the divine Mother and the letters **MP, ΘY**.

17. The priest should not omit remembrance of the saint or saints appointed in the Menaion.

18. Or from the prosphoras given by the faithful for the Liturgy of Preparation, or from individual prosphoras specially prepared for this purpose.

19. As to the taking of particles for the living and of the dead from one and the same prosphora given by worshippers, this is nowhere forbidden and is for all practical purposes expected.

20. According to tradition, this taking of the particles for all whom the priest is called upon to pray is accompanied by the words: *Remember Lord, all who I the unworthy am called upon to pray for, may they not be remembered for what evil they have done in knowledge or in ignorance, or for their many offenses, O Lord, but remember them all, the greatest and the least.*

21. [This prayer is said at all blessings of incense.— *Sluzhebnik*]

22. In some traditions the priest kisses the incensed star, and does the same with the small veils and the aër.

23. The Russian *Sluzhebnik* fails to mention these last words.

24. Taking the veil to cover the paten (and also that for the chalice), and fumigating it in this way, needs to be done properly because, for example, in the autumn the veils can harbor insects. The same should be done with the aër.

25. He censes at the words *In the tomb* from the west, *in hell* from the south, *on the cross* from the east, and *on the throne* from the north.

26. With this difference: that he first censes the table of preparation and then the high place; the opposite order to Vespers.

27. There are four common practices at these prayers: (a) four bows: at *O Heavenly King,* on *Glory to God* (two bows), and on *O Lord, thou shalt open my lips;* (b) three bows: at *O Heavenly King,* once at the double saying of *Glory to God,* and a third at *O Lord, Thou shalt open my lips;* (c) three bows: at *O Heavenly King,* the second and third at each *Glory to God,* no bow at *O Lord, Thou shalt open my lips;* (d) three bows: no bow at *O Heavenly King,* two bows at *Glory to God,* and then at *O Lord, Thou shalt open my lips.*

28. Commonly, he kisses the priest's hand and then goes around the holy table, bowing to the high place and the priest from the northeast corner.

29. In some places where an archimandrite or mitered archpriest serves, the deacon, before he goes out to the solea, opens the holy doors, and the liturgy is begun with the doors open.

30. [The ambo is that part of the solea that extends out into the nave of the church, hence the distinction.—Ed.]

31. I.e., the altar, or holy table. The reference is to the ark of the covenant and the throne of the cherubim found in the First Temple.

32. According to the *Chasoslov* and the *Heirmologion*, they are sung in the eighth tone; in the musical tradition they are sung in the first tone (troparion mode) or in the tone of the week.

33. Sung in the tone of the week.

34. Often, this response is joined to *Both now and ever* at the end of the psalm, in which case the second choir begins with the first verse, and both responses are sung together.

35. In another tradition, at the time of singing *Glory...* on the Beatitudes (i.e., if the troparia are sung).

36. Nowadays, these troparia are normally read by the reader, or omitted altogether.

37. When the troparia are omitted, so also are *Glory...* and *Both now...;* the Beatitudes concluding with *Rejoice and be exceeding glad.*

38. If the troparia are not sung, it is better to begin to make the bows and the Little Entrance quite early on in the singing of the Beatitudes.

39. In some churches, he stands below the ambo, at the side of the right kliros.

40. If the first candle bearer goes on to the ambo, then the second does so as well. If they come down, the second stands by the side of the left kliros facing the first candle bearer.

41. If time is pressing, the diaconal exclamation and the priestly prayer of the Entrance may be said when going from the holy table around the sanctuary to the solea.

42. According to the *Sluzhebnik*, Alleluia follows the entry verse; it should be sung just once, but in some musical traditions, it has come to be sung three times.

43. If the candle bearers stand below the ambo, then at this time they mount the solea and stand before the holy doors.

44. After this the candle bearer (or candle bearers), standing the candlestick near the iconostasis (i.e., between the holy doors and the icons), extinguishes the candle and goes into the altar by the south door. (If there is a second candle bearer, he does the same but on the north side.)

45. If the church is dedicated to Christ or to an event in the life of Christ, then the troparion is not sung. If the church possesses altars to other feasts or saints, then are sung the troparion and kontakion of the altar at which the liturgy is celebrated.

46. If there are several saints of the day, then the troparia are sung in order of seniority, from the greatest to the least.

47. If there are several saints, then the greatest first, *Glory*... and the kontakion of the lesser.

48. In a church dedicated to Christ, the Resurrection Kontakion in the appointed tone is sung instead of *Protection of Christians*, changing it to here from its usual place. In a church of the Mother of God, the kontakion of the church is sung instead of *Protection of Christians*.

49. Normally, the priest only kisses the edge of the holy table; at this point, however, in some traditions, he kisses the Gospel book as well.

50. According to another tradition, the reader goes out carrying the Epistle book leaning against his chest, supported by the left hand.

51. If serving, for example, in a rural church where the only reader is the *psalomshchik,* he must read the Epistle and sing the prokeimenon in place of the choir. In that case, he sings the prokeimenon at the kliros and then goes to read the Epistle.

52. According to the opinion of the esteemed Russian [actually Belarussian.—Ed] liturgist, M. Skaballonovich, the Typikon literally requires the full singing of both prokeimena, the first and the second being sung with their verses, that is the first twice and the second two and a half times.

53. If there are two Epistle readings, the reader only announces the title of the first but puts an inflection in his voice at the beginning of the second.

54. If there are three readings, the reader again announces only the title of the first. The first and the second are read as though one, and the third without title but with an inflection at the beginning.

55. According to the Typikon, the incensation is made after the reading of the Epistle, during the singing of *Alleluia,* but nowadays, due to the style of singing, the censing is done during the Epistle.

56. In several places, when the deacon goes to the analoy, the first (northern) candle bearer goes before him and the second (southern) candle bearer goes behind him; they go around the place where the analoy is, the deacon coming to a stand between them. In this manner, the candle bearers complete their movement so as to each stand in his own place, placing their candles beside the analoy and facing each other.

57. He stands the Gospel book on the part of the table nearest its upper edge, but not in the middle of the table, in case it should fall upon the vessels with the Holy Gifts.

58. There are different traditions concerning the opening and closing of the holy doors in the period

between the reading of the Gospel and the singing of the Cherubic Hymn: (1) Leave the holy doors open until the end of the Cherubic Hymn; (2) close them after the reading of the Gospel (i.e., for the Litany of Fervent Supplication), to be opened only at the Great Entrance; (3) close them after the Litany for the Departed, to be opened at the Great Entrance; and (4) close them after the Litany of Fervent Supplication and open them at the Great Entrance.

59. Petitions for any special needs of the worshippers may be made during the Litany of Fervent Supplication (see the notes to the Great Litany) after the petition *Again we pray for this country*... Also any particular special prayers may follow this litany. When the holy doors are opened (if that be the practice), the deacon: *Let us pray to the Lord;* people, *Lord have mercy;* and the priest says the prayer.

60. The deacon enters the sanctuary by the holy doors (if they are open) or by the south door. In some churches, even when the doors are open, the deacon goes into the sanctuary by the south door.

61. I.e., with the prayer: *We offer Thee incense*....

62. Through the holy doors or the north door. In some churches, the holy doors are opened especially for the Litany for the Departed.

63. A nomocanon in the *Great Trebnik* prohibits the saying of the Litany for the Departed in Sunday services, but in the universal practice of the Russian church and in accordance with the legislative acts of the Church of Constantinople (e.g., the 1807 decree of the patriarchal synod of Constantinople), this practice is permitted. This is stated here because of the inappropriately categorical statements made by some writers on the Orthodox divine services that this litany is forbidden at a Sunday Divine Liturgy.

64. By the holy doors or the south door.

65. Catechumens: those who have not yet received holy Baptism, but who believe and who are preparing for the mystery of Baptism.

66. In another tradition, by the south door.

67. If the church has two choirs, then either one sings the whole hymn, or it is sung in two parts, the first choir singing: *We who in a mystery...,* and the second: *That we may receive...* after the Great Entrance.

68. The traditions agree that the deacon stands to the right of the priest.

69. According to one tradition, they both go directly to the table of preparation. In a second tradition, the priest goes directly to the table and the deacon goes around the table.

70. According to one tradition, when taking the paten upon his head, the deacon kisses its edge.

71. In some churches and dioceses, it is normal for the chalice to be carried over the heads of the faithful. In such a case, the candle bearers must take particular care that people do not pull at the priest and his vestments nor get in his way.

72. In monasteries, the name of the archimandrite or hegoumen of the monastery is remembered after the name of the diocesan bishop, or the name of the abbess in a women's monastery. The name of the diocesan bishop is not pronounced in stavropegial monasteries.

73. At this point, in one tradition, he signs the worshippers with the chalice (from left to right). In a second tradition, he makes the sign of the cross with the chalice. In a third tradition, the worshippers are not generally blessed with the chalice.

74. In some churches, when going into the sanctuary the priest says: *Those who labor and those who sing and all*

the people here present, may the Lord God remember in His kingdom, now and ever, and to the ages of ages.

75. According to another tradition, he places the veils on the upper left side of the table.

76. In another tradition, he does all this only after the Holy Gifts have been covered with the aër.

77. The singing of the Cherubic Hymn should be completed by the time the deacon goes out from the sanctuary to the solea for the Litany of Supplication, so as to avoid a pause in the service.

78. According to the Typikon, the Rector reads the Creed. In practice, where there is a choir, it is sung by them and often also by the people.

79. In another tradition, the hands are not lifted up, and in a third tradition, the right hand only is lifted up.

80. In another tradition, it is folded and put in the same place.

81. In another tradition, he makes a sign of the cross when elevating the gifts.

82. That is why it is desirable that the particles in honor of the Mother of God, the nine orders of saints, and those for the living and the departed, should be a little way from the Lamb and not touching it.

83. According to the Typikon, the deacon, standing in his place, takes a fan, kissing the image of the cherubim on it, and holding it in the right hand with the stole over it, while balancing the shaft in his left hand, makes a sign of the cross a few times with it over the Holy Gifts. (He extends the fan first over the holy chalice and then over the holy paten, then he lowers it between the holy vessels at the side where the tabernacle is and, after that, brings it to the front side of the holy table.)

84. In one tradition, this censing is made as follows: once to the paten, once to the chalice, another to the paten, and

another to the chalice, and then one more time toward the paten and chalice together.

85. In one tradition, the deacon also censes the high place and the icons in the sanctuary.

86. According to the Typikon and the old chant books, in the tone of the week, but now most usually *It is truly meet...* is sung in the eighth tone, and often sung with the people.

87. During this prayer, the priest may remember by name those of the dead whom he wishes.

88. The deacon, having finished censing the holy table, makes his own commemorative prayer for those who have fallen asleep.

89. During this prayer, the priest may remember by name those of the living whom he wishes.

90. If the deacon conducts the people during the singing of the Lord's Prayer, this arranging of the stole is done after the exclamation: *Through the grace and compassion....*

91. According to several rubrics, with three fingers of both hands.

92. The Lamb is removed from among the particles to the Mother of God and the nine orders of saints by the priest lifting it with both hands, saying aloud *The holy things....* He then briefly holds it with one hand, while with the other, he brushes aside with the sponge all the extracted particles to the lower edge of the paten. He then immediately starts the breaking of the raised Lamb.

93. According to the Greek Typikon and chant books, and also in the tradition of the Slavonic church, the Sunday communion chant is sung in the tone of the week. Nowadays in the Russian church, it is sung to a special melody.

94. If there is a special service of prayer (the purpose of which was mentioned in the great and insistent litanies)

and the proper Epistle and Gospel appointed were read, then after the communion verse of the saint, they sing that of the special service.

95. There is a tradition whereby after singing *Alleluia* three times, the irmosy and stichera of the feast are sung, or the prayers before Holy Communion are read. It is better if the period between *The holy things are for the holy* and *With fear of God...* is entirely filled up with the communion verse.

96. If there is only the Sunday communion verse, then that is sung by the first choir and the threefold *Alleluia* by the second choir. If there is also a communion verse of a saint, the choirs alternate among themselves, and the threefold *Alleluia* is completed by the choir whose turn it is.

97. Dividing the Holy Bread into four parts along the lines of the incisions made earlier.

98. The portion **IC** is placed in the chalice by the priest; the portion **XC** will be to communicate himself and the deacon who serves with him, and the portions **NI** and **KA** to communicate the people.

99. With the thumb and index finger of the right hand.

100. Placing as much of his hand into the chalice as may be necessary to place the portion gently into it.

101. The server must be careful to pour in sufficient water when it is very hot or even boiling.

102. According to another tradition, this bow is not made.

103. In a second tradition, this bow to the ground is made when saying *Loose, remit...;* in a third, it is a bow from the waist. [It may be noted that the prayer *Loose, remit...* is not found in the *Sluzhebnik.*—Ed.]

104. In another tradition, they say: *Forgive me, fathers and brothers, in all that I have sinned before you, in word, in deed, in thought and in all my senses.* [This is also not in the *Sluzhebnik.*—Ed.]

105. [This dialogue is not in the *Sluzhebnik.*—Ed.]

106. In another tradition, the deacon starts to say the prayer *I believe, O Lord, and I confess*... not at the north (or east) side of the table, but as soon as he leaves to go there.

107. It is necessary to be especially vigilant that no drop of the Holy Blood is left on the lips or beard of the celebrating clergy.

108. If there are no communicants, then the deacon now holds the paten over the chalice and puts the Holy Body into the chalice, the portions of the Lamb not being further broken, and all the other particles as well, saying the appointed prayers.

109. He leaves the candle lit, placing the candlestick to the right of the preparation table.

110. In another tradition, the deacon holds the chalice, and the priest holds the spoon (with which communion is given) and the cloth.

111. Wine with water and blessed bread.

112. This applies to children up to age seven.

113. Instead of *Servant of God*, he may say *child*.

114. In several traditions, when the chalice is held by the deacon, the mouth of the communicant is wiped by the priest or the server.

115. In another tradition, the priest, having communicated the laity, signs them with the chalice, saying: *This has touched your lips, and shall take away your iniquities, and cleanse you from your sins. Alleluia, Alleluia, Alleluia.*

116. If the chalice was held by the deacon, then he gives it to the priest, and the priest, taking it, kisses it.

117. In some traditions, this exclamation is pronounced at the holy doors.

118. [The words "the Mother of God" are not in the *Sluzhebnik*. —Ed.]

119. In one tradition, the priest makes a sign of the cross with the chalice at these words.

120. Traditionally, this litany is pronounced in the same way as the Short Litany after the hymn *Only-begotten Son...,* i.e., the deacon chants the first two petitions as one and the choir sings *Lord have mercy* (twice) during this.

121. If this is sung antiphonally, the first choir, then the second, and then again the first.

122. In one tradition, this psalm is substituted by the reading of the Prayers of Thanksgiving after Holy Communion, in another by any moleben, and in a third, it is omitted entirely.

123. In practice, the chalice is wiped dry with a communion cloth.

124. Traditionally, after the saint of the church, those of importance in that locality.

125. The priest gives this dismissal at the holy doors facing the people, holding the precious cross in his hands.

126. Following the order appointed in the *Sluzhebnik.*

127. Before removing his vestments, the deacon extinguishes the lights on the holy table and on the table of preparation and covers them (the holy table and preparation table) with a cloth.

Chapter 4: The Liturgy of the Presanctified Gifts

1. In practice, the entry prayers are done at the end of the Ninth Hour, so that during the Typika the clergy can be vested in time to pray the Prayer of St Ephrem the Syrian.

2. In past times, and according to earlier practice described in our *Sluzhebnik*s, the Presanctified Gifts were to be found upon the table of preparation. Then, where such practice obtained, the priest, following the directions of the *Sluzhebnik,* went to the table of preparation, and,

"taking the censer, censes the ark with the Holy Gifts, and making a bow to the ground, opens the ark, and, taking the Holy Presanctified Lamb, places it with great reverence on the paten, saying nothing, only *Let us pray to the Lord: Lord have mercy.* After this, he pours the wine and water into the chalice; covers with the star, small veils, and aër, and, pronouncing these prayers, he places before the Holy Gifts a candlestick with a lighted candle, and, making once more a bow to the ground, goes back to his place, the deacon, taking the censer from him, censes the sanctuary and the whole church." [The editor knows of at least one church in the United States that follows this practice.]

3. Directions for the preparation of the Lamb are found in the *Sluzhebnik* and in modern editions of the liturgy such as that of St Stephen's Press (Oxford: 2002), i–iii.

4. In some places, in agreement with old customs, this rite is preserved as the way in which the early Christians brought the evening light into the assembly of prayer. The priest leaves the sanctuary through the holy doors carrying the candlestick that stood before the table of preparation, leaving it on the solea. After *O Jesus Christ, Thou gentle light* and *Peace be with all,* the candle bearer bows to the priest, who is standing at the high place, and takes it into the sanctuary. The same is done when there are two candle bearers (as in current practice): They take out the candlesticks, standing with them before the solea until the conclusion of *O Jesus Christ, Thou gentle light* and *Peace be with all,* after which, bowing to the priest and each other, they carry the candles into the sanctuary.

5. According to the Typikon, the first and last *Let my prayer . . .* and all the verses are sung by the serving priest, standing before the table and censing. However, it is also

now common for *Let my prayer...* to be sung in the center of the church by three singers.

6. [NB: The priest does not go about the holy table during this censing.—Ed.]

7. If more than one priest serve, the most senior takes the paten with the Holy Gifts; the second, the chalice; the third, the cross; and so on, as at a full liturgy.

8. This direction of the *Sluzhebnik* needs to be kept in mind, that the deacon does not carry the paten as at a full liturgy. According to established practice, the deacon holds the censer in his right hand and in his left a candle. If two deacons serve, the junior goes first with the candle, and after him the senior with the censer, continually censing the Holy Gifts; both face the Holy Gifts.

9. The practice described here is that of the contemporary Russian church and is the same as that laid down by the *Sluzhebnik* and in the liturgical books produced by the Orthodox Church in America (*Service Books of the Orthodox Church,* Volume 2 (South Canaan, Pa.: St Tikhon's Press, 1984), 155–6. By contrast, a typical modern Greek *Hieratikon* (Athens: Apostolike Diakonia, 1992) 218, requires the formula *The fullness of the Holy Spirit* to be said when the portion ΙΣ is placed in the chalice, and the rubrics expect the priest and deacon to receive communion in the normal way. The "fullness" formula is also found in other and older sources, e.g., the Moghila *Sluzhebnik* of 1639 (reprinted Lvov and Fairfax, Va., 1996, 662ff.). This book, often thought to be a Latinizing work, expects both priest and deacon to receive from the chalice with the usual formula referring to the Precious Blood. These two examples witness to the older tradition that saw the chalice as having been consecrated by contact with the presanctified Lamb. The Latin influence that led to the present Russian practice is therefore of late date and should

probably not be regarded as doctrinally binding. The editor would, however, counsel clergy considering change to not do so without asking the blessing of their bishops. The contemporary unwillingness in the Russian church to communicate infants at this service stems from the same understanding.

10. Infants, insofar as they are not able to take a particle of the Body of Christ, are not communicated at the Liturgy of the Presanctified Gifts.

11. [Although they are often found in modern editions.—Ed.]

12. The Kiev Caves Monastery was in the habit of celebrating the presanctified daily, Monday to Friday, excepting only the Monday and Tuesday of the first week (see Fr K. Nikolsky, *Uchebnyj Ustav Bogosluzheniya* [reprinted Moscow: 1999], 476, footnote 1). The present practice of the monastery is not known to the editor.

Appendix 1: Vestment Colors

1. Directions for the vestment colors set forth here are in accordance with ecclesiastical practice, and according to the chapter in Vol. 4 of *The Handbook for the Clergy* (Nastol'naya Kniga Svyashchennika: Moscow, 1983) entitled "The Colour of the Vestments for Divine Service: The Symbolism of the Colours."

2. Actual practice is to celebrate services in honor of the Cross of Christ in claret-colored vestments or in those of red color, but of a much darker shade than the paschal red.

3. In olden times, the Orthodox Church did not use black vestments at all, and during the Great Fast served in "crimson robes," i.e., dark claret. One might celebrate in such a way on the Lenten weekdays by using violet vestments, but of a darker shade than those worn on the Lenten Sundays.

4. [Other authorities, red.—Ed.]

5. [Bright red is the Russian custom, based on the play on the words "red" and "beautiful"—this does not have the same resonance in English (or even Ukrainian), and white is more commonly used, although bright red vestments shot with white or silver would be very suitable for Pascha.—Ed.]

6. According to common current practice, throughout the whole Dormition Fast (excepting Transfiguration), robes of light blue color are used.

7. The vestments on weekdays are changed to the color corresponding to the saint named, when the service of the saint is of Polyeleos or Great Doxology rank. In prefestal periods, the color of the vestments used for celebrating saints of Polyeleos rank is not changed in many churches. When there is a coincident commemoration of a saint on a Sunday, the color of the vestments is not changed and remains gold.

8. On days commemorating Holy Princes who have taken the monastic habit (e.g., the holy great Prince Daniel of Moscow), the divine service is celebrated in green vestments. The service in honor of holy prince-martyrs or passion bearers is celebrated in the vestments for martyrs.

Appendix 2: Complete Collection of Canon Responses

1. From I.V. Gaslov, *Pravoslavnoe Bogosluzhenie: Prakticheskoye Rukovodstovo dlya Klirikov i Miryan* [*Orthodox Divine Service: A Practical Handbook for Clergy and Laity*] (St Petersburg: Satis, 1998), 191–3.

2. [It should be remembered that whereas in Western tradition any non-martyr may be called a confessor, in the Orthodox Church the title is used for one whose confession of faith entailed some measure of suffering.—Ed.]

Appendix 3: Notes for Concelebration by Priests in the Absence of a Bishop

1. The clergy should not form a semi-circle in the church, which simply interposes a barrier of clerical backs in front of the other worshippers.

2. The chief celebrant alone kisses the Gospel book.

3. Volume 1 (Moscow: Patriarchal Publishing House, 1982), 94.

INDEX